REMINISCENCES OF A LANCE-CORPORAL OF INDUSTRY

BY

EDWARD BARFORD

ELM TREE BOOKS

HAMISH HAMILTON · LONDON

First published in Great Britain, 1972
by Elm Tree Books Limited
90 Great Russell Street, London, W.C.1
Copyright © 1972 by Edward Barford
SBN 241 02162 6

Typesetting by Gloucester Typesetting Co. Ltd.,
and printed by Ebenezer Baylis and Son Limited,
The Trinity Press, Worcester, and London

I am much indebted to my secretary, Mrs. Joan Kent, for her
splendid help over this book

CONTENTS

	From the Writer to the Reader	I
	Introduction	3
ONE	MY INTRODUCTION TO BUSINESS	5
TWO	START OF AVELING-BARFORD	27
THREE	NEARLY BANKRUPTED	48
FOUR	MECHANIZING THE INFANTRY	53
FIVE	I ATTEMPT THE IMPOSSIBLE	62
SIX	AVELING-BARFORD OPERATIONS	81
SEVEN	A BIG GOVERNMENT OFFER	86
EIGHT	EDDISON PLANT	93
NINE	ALAN GOOD	98
TEN	POLITICAL VIEWS	104
ELEVEN	ANECDOTES, FUN, PEOPLE OF ACHIEVEMENT (together with the author's views on more weighty matters)	125
	EPILOGUE	182

From the Writer to the Reader

ALMOST all this book has been dictated entirely from memory; usually during the odd half hour at the end of a day's work for my secretary and myself.

I did not look back at what had already been typed – I went forward. Neither did I delve into a large filing cabinet containing a mass of old correspondence, notes, newspaper cuttings, and the like.

The happenings that I relate are graven into my memory. The story is there and I have written it from my heart – in the hope that it may be of interest and perhaps help to younger men.

Nevertheless I apologize now for any sins of omission or commission – also for my earthy and bawdy language – but anything else would not be me.

I have enjoyed working on this book, which has revived memories of old ambitions and crises. Any profits I make from it will be divided into three parts and distributed as follows:

1) To an Eye Research Unit to be selected by Lorimer Fison of Harley Street, a leading oculist, in affectionate remembrance of the late Sir Benjamin Rycroft who devoted his life to eye sufferers without any regard whatever to his own well-being or health.

2) To King Edward VII Hospital for Officers "Sister Agnes", London.

3) To the "Not Forgotten" Association (Veterans of the First World War).

I have always been amused and intrigued by the way in which some men, who have risen from life's ranks in business, are respectfully referred to as Captains of Industry.

I do not think of myself as a captain, or even as a lieutenant of industry. I am content to have escaped from the position of private: lance-corporal is the rank that suits my temperament. It is, I believe, the rank that Napoleon was proudest of achieving; and, like Mahommed's coffin, it is neither too high nor too low. Hence my choice of title for this book.

One more thing. During the past few years, I have seen how in this country, and no doubt in others, the feeling has spread that people, as individuals, can do little to change the mind and direction of governments. "They", the faceless ones, seem to be in overall and immutable control.

This, of course, is no new belief. I have encountered such defeatist thought in business and in politics from the earliest days of my involvement in these two, sometimes parallel, activities. But it is a wrong view, as I think my own story shows. For if sufficient people feel strongly enough about anything, their will can become a lever to move events their way – if they push hard enough.

As I look back over two world wars, through a slump, depression, and more recent booms and recessions, I see how, time and again, events and situations have repeated themselves. Yet very few people seem able to take advantage of this historical repetition, either in their own lives or in the destinies of nations. They wait for others to give them a lead, to point the way for them when, instead, they should be following their own stars.

Of all Aesop's fables, there is one which, as a manufacturer of heavy earth-moving equipment for so many years, I find particularly apt so far as this attitude is concerned.

A waggoner on a lonely road found that his wheels sank into the mud up to their axles. Immediately, he fell to his knees and prayed to Hercules, the god of strength, to pull him out of the mess.

But Hercules replied in words that are as true today as ever they were: "Put your own shoulder to the wheel. The gods help those who help themselves."

INTRODUCTION

MOST autobiographies deal with men who have become such outstanding successes that their names are already well known before they ever begin to write.

Newspapers, television, and periodicals have made the highlights of their careers and achievements common knowledge, so that to tell the story of their lives is largely a matter of filling in the gaps between one achievement and the next.

Certainly, these stories make interesting reading, but the average reader probably does not feel that the achievements described have any analogy to his own run-of-the-mill life. And even if the great man started poor, the ordinary reader does not see how he could possibly emulate such success in his own chosen sphere.

Such stories have nothing to teach him, no lesson that can be brought to bear on his own problems, his own life; they do not inspire him with confidence that he could do the same.

Also, such autobiographies carefully omit early struggles and setbacks, and very seldom do they describe the one important rung in the ladder that marked the first step from obscurity to achievement.

Thus, after a few references to the writer's early days, the young man jumps from 10s. a week to a scale of activity that suggests he has already accumulated £100,000 or more.

Many people agree that if a man can turn the traditional £50 into £100,000 in a few short years, then he has learned enough by hard and often bitter experience to multiply this £100,000 into several millions far more easily, and with much less pain. But these accounts do not explain how this was done.

This story is not like that.

This is a story about me; an ordinary and unexceptional man, who made many mistakes, but who came through all right in the end. I am completely unknown to the general public, and rightly so. There is nothing spectacular about me or my modest achievements.

3

I started in business with debts of £4,000 and no assets whatever. Before I had made any capital these debts had risen to £7,000 which is £42,000 at today's values. And I did finally achieve a certain success, in spite of many major errors and mistakes.

What I have done, I am sure that literally scores of thousands of others can do in their own spheres, if they are so minded. Thus I have set down each step I took, each rung in the ladder, and when I made a mistake I do not gloss it over.

I hope, therefore, that my story will appeal to the scores of thousands of ordinary men in ordinary streets who feel that they are capable of striking out on their own, but who have hitherto been nervous or otherwise reluctant to take such a serious step.

The first few steps to independence are the most difficult and require the most courage. But once a man takes the initial two or three steps up the ladder, he finds life far more interesting and challenging, and infinitely more rewarding.

I speak of what I know, for had I not received a measure of business success myself, I would never have found myself in the position of what was, in effect, trying to set the stage single-handed for a General Election!

But more of that in its place.

E.B.

London, W.1
January 1972

CHAPTER ONE

MY INTRODUCTION TO BUSINESS

I SUPPOSE I took my early upbringing for granted in the same way as almost every other small boy. You were there, a small boy of, say, five or six, in a family of five children, with a mother and father, more or less unaware that other families were less important, equal, or more important. It was all ordained and ordered, and you did what you were told (more or less), and if it was less you got punished, as you well knew you would be.

Today, I look back and realize that my forbears for a number of generations had been bound up with English soil and that our family fortunes (or lack of them) went up and down together with those of everyone else involved with feeding the families of England.

I don't know where we ranked socially, and I don't think anyone particularly cared – a largish comfortable home, servants in the house, garden, and stables. Cookie supplied us all with plenty of nourishing food. A governess came to teach my elder brother and me something of the three Rs before we were packed off to a preparatory school near Broadstairs. I think I was then nearly eight years old.

My father, James Golby Barford, was at this time half owner of Barford & Perkins Ltd. of Peterborough, manufacturers of certain types of agricultural machinery – in some of which they were among the leaders. Founded well before 1840, they were one of the country's oldest engineering companies, and although small it was the largest employer in the then smallish town.

The early proprietors of whom one was my grandfather were largely responsible for the first two open public spaces – the Stanley Recreation Ground and the Public Park. Old records show that my grandfather invented, about 100 years ago, a system of steam ploughing known as the roundabout system, with which only one huge steam ploughing engine was required instead of two. He also invented water ballasting, then used in horse-drawn rollers and smaller ones down to garden rollers.

His heavy involvement in fox hunting and his love of it had led him into designing and manufacturing steam cooking equipment for the better and easier preparation of food for packs of fox-hounds. In turn, this led him to conceive the idea of an annual foxhound show, which he naturally sited at Peterborough.

The Peterborough Foxhound Show is still very much alive, and is the only one in England, and perhaps in the world, so far as I know. The principal founders were named as the then Duke of Beaufort and Alderman William Barford, JP of Peterborough, and his several enthusiastic associates. When the show was firmly established some years later, about 1893, a large number of fol-lowers of foxhounds throughout England thanked the founder and my grandfather received a silver bowl suitably inscribed, "Presented to William Barford Esq. Chairman of the Peterborough Agricultural and Hound Show Societies this bowl, a tea and coffee service, a watch and chain and a sum of money invested by him in the funds of the Royal Agricultural and Benevolent Institution by members and friends 10 July 1894."

Makers of equipment or machinery to help food production were in a special class of their own. Ploughs had been invented thousands of years before, probably in mid-Europe, but by about the turn of the nineteenth century England was emerging as a farming country containing individuals experimenting with mech-anical aids to the squire, the tenant farmer, and his lads (of all ages) who produced the basic necessity of life – food. Food and clean water have always been just that; no more, no less.

The public display of all the brainwork, research, and physical effort that went into farming and food production was then largely centred in the annual Royal Agricultural Show, held at half a dozen regular sites in rotation in various parts of England, where improvements in farming methods, early ideas on rotation of crops and the evolution of fertilization were discussed.

Naturally the show soon included cattle displays and ideas for improvements to stock rearing, and to the spectators' delight there was a horse ring where hacks, hunters, jumpers were both displayed and judged. Packs of foxhounds also paraded in the ring, together with displays by some of the finest whips in Britain, driving anything from a four-in-hand to a light gig with a pony between the shafts. Martial music, from massed regimental bands, and four-ale bars, made a day's outing to the Royal an attraction to scores of thousands of people who really were not quite certain where a cow keeps her udders.

There is a painting of my umpteenth grandfather standing in the judging ring about 150 years ago. Valentine Barford was actually judging pedigree sheep, which doesn't sound the tops. But he is exquisitely attired in black frock coat, tight trousers, patent leather black boots with contrasting tops and buttons, a silk hat of the period, a large gardenia in his buttonhole, and carrying a pair of grey gloves in the hand which held his gold mounted ebony cane.

The poor chap must have been sweating like a pig but he was judging sheep!

I don't know how many years elapsed before the Smithfield Club and its annual show of livestock and farming machinery was started, but my forbears were also concerned with that. It was held in late November each year in the old Agricultural Hall at Islington, London. My forbears were paid a compliment in that the short side street built to service the hall was named Barford Street. This only disappeared when the whole site of this fine example of the architecture of those days was demolished for redevelopment.

The Smithfield Show still flourishes, of course, at Earls Court, and the family connection is preserved through the work of my elder brother, Geoffrey, who had carried on the family tradition and was President of the Royal Smithfield Club in 1959. A deputy lieutenant for the county of Lincolnshire, he has also been a leading figure and has done much sterling work in the Royal Agricultural Society.

Before I could begin to take an active interest in the company the First World War was upon us, and I joined up as soon as I was old enough, going straight into the army from Rugby School.

I came out of it a crock, and spent over two years in military hospitals after being left for dead on falling wounded into a mustard gas shell crater in front of a wood near Cambrai in March 1918. I have no idea how long I lay there because I was unconscious. Probably about forty-eight hours I was told six weeks afterwards.

7

All I remember is recovering enough consciousness to guess that I had been dumped on the "dead waggon" with a large heap of corpses and part-corpses, arms, legs, and trunks. I did not really know what was going on, but I did recover enough savvy to realize that all was not well. On the one hand I felt blissfully free from pain, and I know I did not want to go back to a world that had been such bloody hell almost every hour of every day for so long. On the other hand, I realized that if I didn't make a huge effort to come to I'd be buried alive together with all those corpses and bits of corpses.

Terror gripped me and some of the mist cleared. I managed to move one hand. My face had swollen, as I learned weeks later, to twice its normal size and my eyes were so bunged up with the effects of mustard gas that I must have looked deader than a lot of the corpses.

Then there was the loud authoritative voice of an NCO saying something like: "Hi there, this bloke ain't dead! Lift him off – gently – and lay him by the roadside there. You, stop with him. There's a good overcoat on that one there. Take it off the stiff and cover this officer with it. We'll send the first medical orderly we see back to him pronto. And stop the first bit of transport that looks as if it can squeeze him in."

But the young officer was unconscious again.

It was not until 1923 that I was finally clear of the army. I spent much of those five years going backwards and forwards from medical examination to hospital and back again, for medical treatment. My original 100 per cent disability pension in 1918 had been steadily whittled down until finally in disgust I commuted the remainder for a lump sum of about £500. But it was vitally urgent that I should go into business to earn some money because my father died suddenly in 1923. Apart from the shock of his death, I was dismayed to find that there was no money – but more of this later.

I joined the head office of Agricultural and General Engineers Ltd., to which the family business, Barford & Perkins Ltd., had been sold in 1919. This group, formed immediately after the war, had purchased, in exchange for its own shares, a dozen family engineering businesses and had an issued capital of £8 million. This would be equivalent to about £40 million today. A.G.E. was the largest group of its kind in England in those days. It built and owned Aldwych House and occupied a large slice of the building, including the ground floor as showrooms.

Some very nasty things were to be said about A.G.E. by me some seven years later, and since these nasty things were reported and commented on very fully in the city columns of the national press, it may be of interest to the present generation of professional men, as well as to professional investors of collective funds, if I set down my story of what actually happened. At the time, I was asked to give up a lot of time to be interviewed by officers of the Crown, and did so fairly lavishly. To what extent others also gave their time and were thanked, as I was, "in the public interest", I don't know.

I fancy that A.G.E. must have been only one of the concerns that attracted the attention of the watchdogs of commercial morality, as a year or two later there was some tightening-up of company law.

The chief promoter and first chairman of A.G.E. was a man named Maconochie, of Maconochie Rations fame. He was a man of standing and a director of the Great Eastern Railway Company. He said officially that A.G.E. was being formed to combat the big amalgamations and expansions of agricultural machinery and tractor makers that had taken place in the United States during the war.

That may have been so. But my father, one of the original directors, certainly never told me that the promoters of A.G.E. had helped themselves to a five per cent commission, in shares, on the purchase price of every firm they managed to persuade to join the group. I did not discover this until years later. I had often wondered why some of the member firms had not the remotest connection with agriculture.

The promoters hoped to build A.G.E. into a £30 million group. If they'd succeeded, it would have meant reasonably nice pickings. Their cut would have amounted to a million and a half £1 shares, shares that stood, for a year or two, at 25s. to 27s. 6d. That discovery, on my part, explained a lot of things, most of which are self-evident.

Most of the directors of A.G.E. were the chairmen of member companies, which position they retained as the group was a holding company. Aldwych House Estates Ltd., which owned Aldwych House, was added as another subsidiary.

At some later stage a director of trust companies of the highest integrity and reputation in the City of London represented the preference shareholders. He only attended Board meetings and I am convinced that he knew nothing of the five per cent commission the promoters had voted themselves before he joined the Board.

As his son now occupies an equally exalted position in the City I will not mention his name. He attended a cocktail party or two of mine years ago, but today I do not meet the top city gents as much as I should, and our paths have not crossed.

Descendants of the original directors and of those who filled the vacancies caused by death up to 1930 will forgive me, I hope, when I describe the Board of A.G.E. – the Board consisting, as I say, of chairmen of member companies.

These businesses were among the oldest in England, many of them having been founded at the beginning of the New Iron Age. Barford & Perkins was registered as a company in 1840, but had been in existence long before that. In the Victorian era of great national prosperity all the companies that now formed A.G.E. had expanded greatly. In some cases, not necessarily in the case of the member companies, or even in the case of engineering firms, I am personally convinced these old family businesses prospered mightily in spite of their owners. Grandfathers and great-grand-fathers had done the work and had founded businesses on solid foundations. But long before 1919 they had become country squires and didn't need to go to their workshops more often than they wanted. All they had to do was pick a good manager and leave it to him. If the manager didn't seem to be doing as well as he might, the answer was simple – try another.

In my view those charming gentlemen who came to take such an active part in the affairs of such occasions as, for instance, the Royal Show, neither wished nor cared to delve into matters of business. They had not been trained to, anyhow. It was men like these who found themselves, in 1919, approached by the promoters of A.G.E.

They must have known about this five per cent commission. I seem to recollect my father once casually mentioning that in these big mergers it was the usual thing for the chaps who had done all the work to get a cut.

The method adopted in valuing the old family businesses also tended to obscure, or belittle, any such trifle as payment to the promoters. After all, each of the ruling families was concerned only in what it itself stood to get net in shares for its own business, and how much capital this represented at the current market price of A.G.E. shares.

The private companies had only a minute paid-up capital compared to their real assets and earning power. And very ordinary-looking share certificates, too. Mostly the kind you can buy — blank, of course! — at a suitable stationers. And instead of owning seven or eight thousand shares in the family business, members of these families now owned sixty or seventy thousand shares in what appeared to them a huge and powerful group. And A.G.E.'s share certificates were huge and most impressive-looking, too.

Except that the men who became the first directors of A.G.E. were asked to give their solemn promise not to sell their shares in the Group!

My father, for one, kept his promise faithfully, though he got very worried about A.G.E. during the last year of his life. It was all something, however, that he and the other directors of A.G.E. were simply not qualified or equipped to understand. They thought that mere size brought additional prosperity. The vast and lavishly-equipped head office awed and impressed them. They could not realize that it was all a huge additional load upon the joint profits of the subsidiary companies.

The 1921 slump must have shaken them all badly. By this time Maconochie had faded out. I had not even seen him. His place was taken by a man named G. E. Rowland, who was to figure quite largely in my business life with A.G.E.

I never did fully learn how Rowland got there, but I believe Maconochie wanted to retire and chose Rowland as his successor. About four years later Rowland told me himself that he had made himself a very considerable fortune during and immediately after the First World War, as a company tax expert. He said he "came in" after the auditors of large companies had done their best to see that the company concerned paid no more than its due taxes. Rowland was then engaged on the basis of a ten per cent commission on any further tax savings he could make. In one little job that had not unduly stretched his brains or taken up very much time the saving had been £400,000, so Rowland's commission was £40,000. In spite of being so rich and powerful he was prepared to become full-time Chairman of A.G.E., whose reputation was already, by this time, beginning to get somewhat tarnished.

He had had no hesitation, he told me, in chucking up his lucrative practice as a top tax expert. He had become so rich that money just didn't matter to him any more. But A.G.E. was clearly in a mess, and it would be a national tragedy if the group collapsed, dragging such fine old names and reputations down with it – most of them concerned in the export trade, too. All A.G.E. needed was good firm management from the top, and Rowland gave it just that.

"You must understand," he said, "that many people resent firm rule, even though it's for their own good as large shareholders."

They certainly did, and Rowland was unpopular in the obvious quarters, particularly at the outset of his rule, but within a year or two he had beaten down all opposition and got his fellow directors just where he wanted them. His scorn for them was intense.

He told me all this after I'd been working for the group for four years. He went on to say that he'd been watching my work carefully all that time, during which he'd given me several lucrative, and most welcome, increases in salary. Then he said he needed a personal assistant, and offered me the job – at a salary of £2,250 a year, say the equivalent of £16,000 p.a. in 1972.

This put me £250 a year above the total each director of A.G.E. was allowed to pay himself from his constituent company. Rowland said he couldn't offer me a directorship because of certain original agreements entered into when A.G.E. was founded. But he would see to it that I was in fact, if not in name, number two only to himself, Rowland, and if anyone was so ill-advised as to endeavour to obstruct me whilst I was carrying out Rowland's orders there would be hell to pay.

He need not have been so vehement. One of the first things I'd learned on joining the group in 1923 was that Rowland had whipped his directors into abject submission soon after becoming the boss. They were literally terrified of him, and I'm quite sure that I was too, at that time, though I didn't see him very frequently. The directors behaved like sheep finding themselves in the same cage as a roaring lion.

Rowland's was a tremendous personality, and he dominated the entire scene at Aldwych House. He had a certain sadistic streak which made him whip the weakest just that bit harder. Even more than that, he enjoyed it, in fact he relished, the prospect of battle if ever he sensed that his subjects were whispering together as to how best to overthrow him. His sixth sense seemed to warn him of danger, and he was overjoyed at the opportunity of showing his strength. He was wily, too — a superb tactician. I am sure he sometimes longed for worthier opponents because as it was he only had to use the same tactics every time — "divide and rule" — the details being tailored to suit the circumstances and individuals concerned in each plot to unseat him.

He paid his directors this compliment if no other. He watched them and pigeon-holed in his mind the way they were likely to group, if battle was joined, and how best to set one group against another should the need arise.

I was never at staff college but I'd attended courses which included some strategy and tactics up at Catterick Camp during the periods when I was temporarily out of hospital, and I recognized Rowland's general strategy.

I watched him with fascination and admiration. In a hugely larger sphere he could have been a dictator. He'd have proved a ruthless one.

My first job with A.G.E., in 1923, was in export sales. I knew precisely nothing about exports, or sales, or engineering, or the group's products. I was much depressed until I realized that this was exactly what those around me expected. England was still at the tail end of the feudal system in those days. I had only just left one great feudal organization — the Army. Some were born to be officers and some were born to be other ranks, and everyone agreed that this was right and proper. I have often wondered who the wily cleric was who managed to get the words inserted into the Anglican Church Service about how we should all be happy and content in that state of life to which it has pleased God to call us. There was also the hymn going,

> *The rich man in his castle*
> *The poor man at his gate,*
> *He made them high and lowly*
> *And ordered their estate.*

My name was Barford and although Barford & Perkins Ltd. was the smallest of the member companies it was also the oldest. This seemed to give it a special cachet. The heads of those old family firms were expected to be able to talk in general terms and with suitable gesticulation and emphasis about everything that concerned their business . . . but only to suitable people, who knew what the form was. Never to actual engineers, works managers, or sales managers, people who might ask questions of a technical nature. There were plenty of employees who could be summoned by a wave of the hand to talk to chaps like that.

So it wasn't so bad after all.

And I had another important advantage, although I thought it a grave disadvantage until several years later. So far as I knew then, or subsequently, the Barfords were the only owning family to have no capital or assets outside A.G.E. So as A.G.E. had already stopped paying dividends and the value of its shares had nose-dived, the Barford family was penniless. Naturally, I undertook to support my mother and live on what was left over. Advancement in the group, and all that that implied as regards increases in salary, thus meant a hell of a lot to me. And I worked. I worked very hard, and was soon in charge of the group's export sales to about a third of the globe, including India.

I knew that A.G.E. was doomed. It was only a question of how long. Apart from the salary involved, I knew that those who had done well in A.G.E. would stand the best chances of good jobs in other firms when the crash came. And then came Rowland's offer. I accepted it gladly. What else could I do? I had no City or other connections. No capital, no prospects of legacies, no qualifications.

After taking on the job of Rowland's personal assistant, I really got to know this remarkable man. He had become a big shot in industry generally, prominent in the Federation of British Industries and similar organizations. He was a member of important delegations to tell the Chancellor of the Exchequer and the like just how best to help British industry, in particular the export trade. He was the only link between A.G.E. and its bankers, Barclays. He was the only man who knew Barclays' chairman, Mr. Goodenough. He was the only man who knew his way around the City of London, the Board of Trade, and so on.

Early on, one of my jobs became to sit in for Rowland at those meetings he did not attend himself. I did not say anything, or vote, unless previously instructed by him. These meetings were my first contact with the high-ups of both industry and the government departments, and I was most grateful for the opportunity.

Rowland worked like a black — there is no doubt about that — and he drove me to the limit as well. I didn't mind, though I did not share Rowland's firm belief that he could and would pull the group round. But I did ask for a rise each year. I asked him for £500 each time, and each time I got £250. By the end I was drawing £3,250 a year in salary.

It was now early 1930. Salaries have gone up about seven times since those days, and my salary of £3,250 a year would be about £20,000 today. Not bad, I thought, for a chap of thirty-two with no qualifications whatsoever. I mention these figures only because I think they might be of interest to chaps of that age now.

However, in the ensuing nine months, I had begun to learn, or gravely suspect, a number of disquieting facts. I will mention only the two things which finally brought about the blazing quarrel between Rowland and myself — and my instant dismissal.

The Secretary of Aldwych House Estates Ltd., a man named Knight, came to me in a very disturbed state and asked if he could meet me one evening for a long private talk. He was very agitated and conspiratorial, and he kept glancing at the door — obviously in case Rowland should suddenly walk in.

I met Knight in a quiet restaurant after work that evening. He may have been a qualified accountant. I doubt it, but he was good at figures. He was a few years older than me. He said that for a year or more he had been most worried at the way Rowland was conducting the affairs of Aldwych House Estates Ltd. The worst thing was the debenture on the building, which had been the biggest sum Rowland had been able to negotiate. The Debenture Deed, said Knight, clearly laid down that the first charge on the rents, including that from A.G.E. itself, paid to Aldwych House Estates Ltd. was to be necessary outgoings and running expenses. Rates, taxes, repairs, maintenance generally, porters' and cleaners' wages, followed by debenture interest and amortization.

Knight suspected that his predecessor, financially in a much more secure position than Knight was, had resigned on ethical grounds. Now matters had got much worse. On several occasions

Knight had steeled himself to mention the matter to Rowland, only to receive a blazing ticking-off. And, on two occasions, a rise in salary. A married man with children, Knight could not afford to throw up such a well-paid job and after many sleepless nights had decided to lay the facts before me and be guided by my advice.

Apparently Rowland had made Knight transfer almost all the gross rents paid to Aldwych House Estates Ltd. to A.G.E. as a loan. Accordingly A.G.E. owed its subsidiary a very large sum, for which Knight held proper receipts from Rowland on behalf of A.G.E. But Aldwych House Estates Ltd. had only enough cash to pay weekly wages. Knight was being mercilessly pressed for rates, taxes, repair and maintenance bills, all of them years overdue. Rowland's strict orders were to pay up the very small chaps after a few months and try to stave off writs from the large chaps by paying a bit on account at intervals. Although this plan largely succeeded, the total amount owing was increasing every month and Knight was sick with worry. His wife and his doctor were most concerned, in fact, about his health. He asked me whether he could be held liable in law for just obeying Rowland's orders. Could I find out for him?

I asked if he knew whether the Trustees for the Debenture holders, Sir Herbert Hambling and Lord Bethell, knew anything of this. His answer was no. At the infrequent formal meetings with the Trustees, Rowland's procedure was to have under his blotter a very large cheque from A.G.E. to Aldwych House Estates Ltd., reducing, say to half, the total debt. Knight knew about this and was ordered to stay mum if either of the Trustees asked for any figures. Obviously, Rowland anticipated the possibility of, say, a London branch manager of Barclays learning, in the ordinary course of his business, that one of his customers had a very long overdue account with Aldwych House Estates Ltd., and reporting the matter to his head office. And Sir Herbert Hambling was Vice Chairman of Barclays Bank and Lord Bethell a director. Rowland would not care to be found out by them. So Rowland had taken a risk of telling Knight that if it ever became necessary he would produce this cheque from under the blotter. He had even told Knight the gist of what he would say to the two trustees. As Rowland's proposed story was completely untrue, and as the

Trustees might direct their questions at the Secretary of the Company, Knight, Rowland had to make sure that Knight be so subdued as to listen to Rowland's lies, and even support them, without flinching.

Rowland intended to say that Knight was in poor health and much overworked, as a result of which the financial affairs of Aldwych House Estates Ltd. had got into rather a muddle and payments to creditors were much behind. He, Rowland, had discovered this, by chance, a few days previously and had had some late night sessions with the books of the subsidiary himself. He had thus found out that A.G.E. owed Aldwych House Estates Ltd. a very much larger sum than he had supposed – so that very morning he had made out a cheque putting the subsidiary well in funds again. He would lend Knight one of the bright boys from A.G.E.'s accounts department to get the whole position rectified as soon as possible. At this stage Rowland proposed to produce the cheque, all made out and signed by him, like a conjuror producing a rabbit from his hat.

I told Knight, when I had heard all this, to leave everything to me. I would see him again as soon as possible. As a matter of fact I had already decided that the time for the great showdown with Rowland was very near.

For there was something else I had found out.

This concerned the Export Credits Guarantee Department, which had only been recently established by the Government and was known, for short, as E.C.G.D. The object of the E.C.G.D. was to lend public funds to assist export business by individual firms, and to help finance sales requiring long-term credit. In the preamble to the bulletin then issued by H.M. Stationery Office the word "sale" is clearly defined as meaning, in their words, "firm sale".

The export sales of A.G.E. were all conducted from headquarters at Aldwych House. The group employed, in the capacity of resident representative in the Argentine, a man name Cullington. Goods to the value of perhaps only £20,000 had been shipped to Cullington in his own name, on open consignment. These goods had been put through the group's books, however, as a firm sale to one of the three or four great machinery distributors in the Argentine, and the appropriate funds drawn from the E.C.G.D.

I will not mention the name of the company concerned because it was entirely innocent and its reputation today is as great as it was then.

In this case the amount involved was comparatively small, but I soon realized, being no longer a green office boy, that a really large killing was in the course of preparation.

Some of the group's subsidiaries, notably Howards of Bedford, had huge quantities of unsold machinery in their yards, and much of it was obsolescent, if not obsolete. Howards made ploughs and there were scores and scores of them unsold. The world slump, although we didn't know it at the time, had already started. Enormous quantities of harrows, ploughs, and other orthodox farming implements, together with a lot of machinery from other firms, almost all of it obsolescent, were being shipped to Cullington, again on open consignment, and again appearing in the group's books as firm sales. I had been asked to sign some of the documents involved and had refused point blank – so the situation between my boss and myself was already tense. And that is a mild word to describe it.

I made a formal appointment to see Rowland so that he'd know this was to be no ordinary chat. Like all great leaders, Rowland sensed battle in the air, and he wanted to choose the time and the place to polish off his young upstart assistant.

I knew the technique. He'd already used it successfully in the past to cool the ardour of any of the country chairmen who disagreed with his policies. It was Rowland's habit to make an appointment with the director of one of the member companies in, say, East Anglia, where train services were indifferent, and when the man arrived at the appointed hour Rowland would be "in conference" and unable to see him. The director, who probably wanted to object to Rowland's savage depredations of his firm's working capital, would watch the time slipping by. He'd remember his reserved seat on the only through train home, his car waiting at the station. Also that he'd brought no overnight suitcase. And so the chairman of a subsidiary who had told his colleagues only a couple of days before that he would have it out with Rowland to the last ditch, began to feel his courage oozing out of his boots. Don't laugh, country gentlemen used to wear boots.

Rowland, of course, knew precisely what this chap had come to say and in lighter mood – he had them – had once given me a preview half an hour before the event of what he expected to hear. Then he told me to be present at the interview, but ninety minutes behind schedule. Apart from the actual dialogue, Rowland had anticipated the whole scene perfectly and we exchanged winks on several occasions.

On his own ground the chairman of the member-company was a big bug, grandson or great-grandson of the founder, ex-High Sheriff of the County, Chairman of the Magistrates, a local squire – but to Rowland, on Rowland's ground, he was just pathetic chicken feed to be given a quick dose of high-falutin' tripe – with a wink at me – and packed off to catch his train and be re-united with his family. To his family, at least, he was still a demi-god.

And this was the technique Rowland used with me. It was not until several days had passed that my summons came, at a moment's notice. I had just got back from a business luncheon, entertaining at Rowland's orders.

I just hoped Rowland didn't know he had a coward on the other side of the desk, and confronted him with these two main issues immediately.

First he tried to persuade me I was wrong and even suggested a further increase in salary, but he was a clever man and didn't waste his breath for long on that. He quickly turned to abuse and sacked me on the spot. He asked me to take my personal papers from my desk and leave the building immediately, never to return. He would instruct the commissionaires that I was not to be admitted. The group's solicitors would advise him what payments, if any, other than a month's salary, were due to me, and that would be sent to me at my private address. That was the last I saw of Rowland.

Unfortunately I had been stupid enough during this short, heated interview to mention that I didn't intend to take this lying down and that I would try to see the Trustees for the Debenture holders of Aldwych House Estates Ltd. to tell them my story. The result was that Rowland got his oar in first. Sir Herbert Hambling curtly refused to see me, and it was relayed to me at my flat by one of the many friends I still had at Aldwych House that Sir Herbert, according to Rowland, completely endorsed

Rowland's treatment of me. I went out to see Lord Bethell by appointment at his country home, Bushey Hall. He heard me out, then brought the interview to a speedy close.

Rowland had won the first round.

I decided to do nothing about the Export Credits matter. I was growing up fast. Only public funds were involved, and who cares about public funds? Then, as now, a few score of million pounds down the drain here and there makes no difference to anybody. A few hundred millions on a missile that doesn't work and costs ten times more than the detailed official estimates – so what? The Department itself was entirely in the clear. Rowland was a much respected leader of industry. I felt I should not fare any better than I had with the Aldwych House Trustees.

I was only thirty-two and completely unknown in any form of business outside A.G.E. I had never worked anywhere else, but I was determined that I would stand by my principles even though it probably meant I would lose everything I had so far gained. To me the City was something mysterious and unknown. So I decided to appeal to the shareholders. This was the mother and father of blunders—the ball was at my feet but I didn't know it. (Years later I realized this, though there wasn't the slightest reason for me to suspect it at the time.) I tried to see Mr. Goodenough, the then Chairman of Barclays Bank. I failed to see him. I realized, again years later, that if I could have persuaded some older man of standing and repute to tell Barclays, at Joint Managing Director level, of my allegations, I would subsequently have gained a hearing. But, as I have already said, Rowland kept entirely to himself all contact with the bank, and with the City. Only a woman secretary, who had been with him a long time before A.G.E., was in his confidence, or so I suspected.

In order to appeal to the shareholders I needed a solicitor of considerable standing in the City. I found one in Mr. Clifford-Turner, founder of Clifford-Turner & Company. He was a remarkable man who feared nobody, and I quickly realized that I was in the best of hands. Unfortunately he fell ill and the partner who took his place, was not of Clifford-Turner's calibre. He lacked the latter's confidence when confronted by all the big names Rowland was able to call upon.

I drafted our first circular to the shareholders, with the idea of striking while the iron was hot. We dithered over the wording. Then, fortunately, Clifford-Turner himself came back, and passed my draft of the circular with certain minor modifications. I shot it out straight away, with Clifford-Turner's amendments altered in ink.

And at this point I had a stroke of luck. The city editors noticed my circular to the shareholders and gave it a little publicity. Rowland and his supporters countered quickly but things were said or done on his side which put the city editors' backs up. I never knew precisely what was said in interviews, but what happened is fairly obvious from the turn things afterwards took.

The city editors of the Express group (S. W. Alexander and Bernard Harris), the Daily Mail (Meredith and Williams), and the Times (Mill, I think) were all of the opinion that young Barford should be given a hearing. There was no reason, they said, why the big battalions should want to crush this young man underfoot without his being given a chance to put his side of the story. They published my circular in full, pointing out prominently that the financial record of A.G.E., that great and powerful group, as given in the published balance sheets, was nothing to write home about. They pointed out that shareholders had seen their shares drop from 27s. and over to almost nothing. All could not be well.

Then I had writs served upon me for libel. This was unpleasant.

The battle, if battle it can be called, raged to and fro. My opponents were sitting in Aldwych House using the shareholders' money to employ the best professional advice they could get. I was sitting in the dining room of my flat at 36 Bryanston Court, spending money I hadn't got and incurring printers' bills, professional fees, and even a huge bill for postage stamps. And I had no income at all.

However, the city editors won the day for me. I had been joined by a few of the main board directors, but only by a few. We called a meeting and sent out proxies in the usual form. I went to the meeting, flanked by Sir Gilbert Garnsey of Price Waterhouse & Company, and H. V. Batchelor of Clifford-Turners.

Both on the poll, and on a show of hands, we won hands down. Directly after the meeting Rowland fled from Aldwych House, leaving no address, pausing only in his flight to scoop up all the petty cash.

He had been living in a suite at the Russell Hotel in Bloomsbury, but none of us had ever been there. I suspect that he had a home somewhere else and that his confidential secretary had taken all his papers there in a number of separate loads so that the operation would not be conspicuous to the rest of the staff. He had cleared out of the Russell Hotel also, again leaving no forwarding address.

And that was the end of Rowland as far as A.G.E. or any other public company was concerned. He had vanished into thin air and, over a period of time, his name was removed from his various appointments, such as the Federation of British Industries, as letters to him remained unanswered.

This was the first of my pyrrhic victories. Next morning I returned to Aldwych House to shake all my friends there by the hand.

Rowland's defeat and subsequent flight had, of course immediate and drastic repercussions. Creditors, small and large, began to press very strongly for payment of their long overdue accounts. Within a week or two Barclays Bank, who were owed about £400,000, put in a Receiver. Naturally, the big bugs in the City of London pinned all the blame on me. I say "naturally" because I am sure there were some very guilty consciences in the City after the collapse of A.G.E. The Big Wigs must have realized in their hearts that they had made complete fools of themselves, and the easiest let-out was to turn round and assure everybody that "None of this would have happened but for that young upstart Barford".

As was natural after a period of enormous strain, anxiety, and over-activity in one's brain-box, coupled with practically no fresh air or exercise, I myself felt deflated and listless for several days. But within a week or so I had to pull myself together and face fresh anxieties. These were of course of a financial nature.

I took quick stock of the situation. I had received no salary for five or six months. I found that the sum total of my debts I had incurred in waging this battle on behalf of the group's shareholders amounted to what was to me the staggering figure of nearly £7,000. Mr. Clifford-Turner, great man that he was, reduced his firm's charges to me to 2,000 guineas without my even asking for such a concession, and told me I could take my time paying him by instalments. He also arranged for certain eminent counsel to wait likewise for their fees. But Clifford-Turner & Company had paid out a good deal of the heavy costs of printing the circulars, and a whole heap of assorted items into the bargain, all of which totalled a pretty hefty sum. I had to endeavour to pay him for all these fairly quickly; if I failed to, Clifford-Turner would have been unfair to his partners.

At the very outset of this battle I had made myself personally responsible for the full costs of the campaign. But the sum total was almost double what I had anticipated. I had also hoped from the beginning that others would weigh in and help me out financially. But nobody did. The net result of it all was that my savings were entirely exhausted and I was over £4,000 in debt, with no job, no income, and no assets, not even a fifth-hand car.

I must now interpose a matrimonial note. At the end of 1927 I had married the younger daughter of the late Lord Ashfield. I am pretty certain that Lord Ashfield liked me from the start, though from any parent's standpoint I was a pretty poor match for his daughter. We had hardly discussed my business affairs at all over the years, as I was most anxious not to impose on the fact that I was his son-in-law, but it was obviously my duty to acquaint him with the fact that I was proposing to give battle to my boss and all those who might support him. Lord Ashfield was very much opposed to the action I intended to take. In this he was strongly supported by Sir Ernest Clark, who was then connected with the Underground Railway Group, as it was then. Lord Ashfield also mentioned my intentions to Sir Harry, afterwards Lord, Macgowan, who endorsed the views of the other two.

The City of London being what it is, they were right – and I was wrong. Had I waged a private campaign instead of a public one, I might well have succeeded in reforming the entire group, with a drastic writing-down of capital, in such a way as to leave myself a director and a chief manager, working for a re-constituted board of City men of standing who could have persuaded the main creditors such as large steel groups, to accept a writing-down of say, fifty per cent of A.G.E. debts to them. We could also have arranged for a considerable moratorium before we even started to pay off the much reduced debts at all. We could have emphasized to the creditors that if they pressed their claims in full, A.G.E. would go bankrupt and then none of the creditors would get anything at all. It would, therefore, be good business for them to accept our proposals for a drastic writing-down of debts and a moratorium.

I still don't know why the big city chaps did not do something of this kind on their own. There are rich pickings to be had in any sudden collapse of this nature. I worked on this line very hard and had interviews with a number of people in the City in which I propounded this scheme. Otherwise there would be nothing at all left over for the Ordinary shareholders. But I proposed to create a tiny issue of management shares of say £10,000 in 1s. shares. Since these would only be what is known as "water" or "paper", many years of hard work would have been necessary before these shareholdings came within sight of a dividend. I therefore proposed that these management shares be distributed free to the new management headed by myself. But after only a few weeks it became painfully obvious that I stood no chance. A.G.E. was doomed. I was the marked man who had created all the rumpus in the first place and forced the group into bankruptcy.

The Receiver, a chartered accountant, was a very poor fish. He was an able accountant, but I felt that in his bloodstream figures took the place of rich red blood. At the outset, when I planned to salvage A.G.E. *in toto*, I tried to persuade the Receiver to put me in as Acting General Manager, with two bright young chaps I knew as my personal aides. I told him my plans for getting the creditors to accept a moratorium, for slashing overheads, for closing down, temporarily at any rate, two of the subsidiaries, which were losing money heavily, and for selling, for cash, one of the biggest of the subsidiaries, a business which had always been a fish out of water with A.G.E., and which, I am sure, had only been brought into the group for the sake of the five per cent commission. As Rowland's assistant I knew that a large combine had in fact approached him with an offer for this company, but that Rowland had wanted far too high a price. I planned to re-open negotiations so that the Receiver could sell the firm for a reasonable sum. Barclays Bank, who had put in the Receiver, were owed only £400,000, secured, which was not an immense figure even by the standards of the time. And although the total unsecured debts to the other creditors came to about double that amount it was clear to me that it wouldn't be beyond my powers to pull the group round, to the very great advantage of all concerned, particularly the staff at the twelve factories, men and women whose livelihood and reasonable well-being were in jeopardy. For them I felt very strongly. They had worked well and loyally, and now faced being sacked without a pension and without compensation. Many of the workers were still working, although their pay cheques were two months or so in arrears.

But no. The Receiver decided that the subsidiary companies must struggle along by themselves, and he would put each one up for sale to raise enough cash to pay off Barclays and leave something over to be divided amongst the creditors.

So I abandoned the effort.

What was I to do next? I badly needed a monthly pay cheque.

I had always been much attracted to Fleet Street. I knew that life was short and sharp there, and the devil take the hindmost. But I also knew that life in Fleet Street was never dull and that there were rich prizes for the successful.

I was also very interested, though not so much as in Fleet Street, in Public Relations, which was then in its infancy, a fact that is hard to realize today. Several men, to my personal knowledge, started in those days from scratch and have built up in thirty to thirty-five years what are now apparently prosperous empires housed in large office blocks that are hives of activity.

But these men started from scratch. I would be starting at scratch minus £7,000 — say £45,000 of today's money. It just wasn't on so I stopped cogitating about it.

From now on I would concentrate on the attempt to revive only two of the group's member companies, Aveling & Porter Ltd., and Barford & Perkins Ltd., my own former family firm.

My second scheme, then, was to buy two of the subsidiaries, Aveling & Porter and Barford & Perkins, off the Receiver. Since I now had friends in Fleet Street as well as detractors in the City he eventually allowed me to assume the position of Acting General Manager of both companies. I soon found that I'd given myself an even larger bunch of headaches than I had anticipated, but I had pressed the Receiver hard for the job — at a salary of £1,500 a year, under half of what I'd been earning previously — so there could be no thought of retreat.

As I have already explained, Barford & Perkins had formerly been owned by the two families jointly, but neither had any interest in it now, of course, having sold out lock, stock, and barrel to A.G.E. in 1919. I felt these two firms, Aveling & Porter and Barford & Perkins, would make a suitable combination since they were both largely in the same line of business, namely road rollers. Aveling & Porter had originated the steam roller, in fact, in 1865, but for the last ten or twenty years had been making diesel-engined machines. Barford & Perkins had originated the motor roller in 1904 and were also now producing diesel-engined machines.

I told the Receiver officially of my new plan, and said I hoped to be able to raise enough money to make him a cash bid, as he insisted, for both companies.

CHAPTER TWO

START OF AVELING-BARFORD

MY NEW scheme was only about a sixth the size of my former project to refloat A.G.E., but I was equally confident that I could make a success of it. The first scheme, however, did not require any raising of money by me personally, whereas the new scheme did. The Receiver was interested only in selling the two companies outright, for cash. The reader should be well aware of my cash position by now.

But at this point I learned from my new-found friends in Fleet Street that merchant bankers did exist who had had shares in A.G.E., either on their own account or on behalf of clients, and who had not agreed with Rowland and his City pals that I was to blame for the bankruptcy which had resulted in the loss of every penny of the shareholders' investments. City memories, furthermore, are often short. Some merchant bankers, and their clients — insurance companies, investment trusts, and so on — had taken a keen interest in the affairs of A.G.E. for a short time, while the heat was on, but as soon as the Receiver was appointed and announced his conviction, as he did, that creditors would get little and shareholders nothing they wrote off their losses and busily turned to other ventures and plans.

I culled the names of several potentially friendly concerns, and individuals, and made appointments to go and see them. I could then decide where I went from there.

At the same time I had already drawn up, in what I euphemistically called my office — in fact my own dining room — a short memorandum outlining my plans for the two companies I wished to buy. At the time of the A.G.E. crash I had received a short but kindly note from a man I had never met, a Mr. Charles, later Sir Charles, Palmour, senior partner of Messrs. Whinney, accountants. A telephone enquiry to a friend revealed that this was one of the leading firms and that Mr. Palmour himself was a man of great standing and influence. He readily consented to see me. I gave him signed copies of the audited accounts of Aveling & Porter and Barford & Perkins for the previous years and, after pointing out several factors which seemed to me important, left them with him. The upshot was a fine little brochure, very short and to the point, with figures attached by Messrs. Whinney, Smith & Whinney.

But even the great Charles Palmour could not paint a very happy picture. Both companies were basically sound, and would have shown satisfactory profits in relation to the capital employed, remaining fully solvent, if they had not been connected with A.G.E. and thus fallen under Rowland's domination.

Every two or three months it had been Rowland's custom to have certain figures sent to London for him to study, and after studying them he would make further demands on the company concerned for loans to the parent organization. These loans were in addition to the regular contributions made to head office for expenses, contributions which were in fact trivial compared to the loans enforced by Rowland. The directors of Aveling & Porter and Barford & Perkins had been no stronger than the directors of the other ten companies when it came to resisting Rowland. The result was that when A.G.E. collapsed it owed the two firms I was interested in about £350,000 on account and the two firms themselves owed more than £250,000 to their trade creditors.

The unpaid bills of steel suppliers and a hundred other companies were six months or so overdue, and further deliveries were naturally being held up until substantial payments were received. As a result, our standing stocks of components, like engines, were so reduced that we were losing orders wholesale which we could easily have fulfilled if our suppliers had delivered goods waiting in their own works for dispatch. The suppliers' refusal to dispatch any more goods was of course fully justified, and if the whole of Britain had not been in the trough of the 1930 to 1933 slump they would have cut off deliveries directly payments to them fell more than two months behind. But they were desperately short of work in their own factories, so they continued to deliver. When the holding company collapsed the position, of course, became even worse, as the subsidiary now knew they had no chance of getting back the huge sums that A.G.E. owed to them.

Mr. Palmour's figures looked very gloomy as £250,000 worth of unpaid bills was by far the largest item! This monstrous figure swamped every other single item, fixed assets, land building, plant and machinery, stock in hand. The £250,000 stuck out of our condensed statement of assets and liabilities like a huge swollen sore thumb. Still, we had produced a nice little brochure and it contained all my hopes and dreams. I was proud of it. And as I was now the Acting General Manager it was up to me to hold my head high, because morale amongst all ranks of our staff at Rochester had sunk dangerously low.

Even in the depths of a depression a wide-awake managing director will replace mediocre members of his staff with better men. Managing directors of other firms were doing this, and I lost several of my most reliable chaps. But most of the staff remained loyal, and deputations of them came to see me to say they would carry on as best they could, provided that I could assure them seventy-five per cent of their monthly salaries, in cash, the rest being credited to them for payment when things looked up. I gave them this assurance, and managed to keep my promise because I was able to obtain further support from many of our principal suppliers. Both companies had been their customers for forty or fifty years, and our suppliers had regretted A.G.E. from the start. They had kept in touch with events in A.G.E. over the years. Their travellers were primed with questions to ask when they visited the works, and learned about the huge loans we had been forced to make to the parent company. So I took our suppliers into my confidence. I showed them my little brochure, and they agreed to release certain essential supplies so that we could carry on, provided that our total indebtedness to them did not increase and provided that I started reducing the debts in three months' time. Other suppliers, of course, were not so generous and help-ful, and the fear of receivership hung over my head like the Sword of Damocles. I was determined, too, not to favour the unfriendly at the expense of those who were proving so helpful and kind.

Looking back nearly thirty-five years I can't understand how I managed to pack so much anxious and difficult negotiations into each week of 168 hours. Everyone must have a little sleep, though food, it is true, can be snatched at any odd moment. But I didn't feel much like food. I was tramping the streets of the City of London waving my little brochure and the only result was that the soles of my shoes wore thinner and thinner.

Unfortunately potential backers were only interested in what showed upon paper, under the headings of Profit and Loss, and although I had Mr. Palmour's full support I still couldn't interest anyone in the companies' future. My story was too complicated, and anyway it was challenged by Rowland's ex-supporters in the City. At every interview I had to give long verbal explanations. The reader must remember that I had received a lot of publicity in the national press during my still recent fight with Rowland, and although events, and the Receiver's report had vindicated me and castigated Rowland, the latter's former supporters had me to thank for the limelight A.G.E. and its dealings had received. They were naturally anxious to play down as far as possible their former association with the group, but that didn't lead them to relish the idea of having anything to do with me. I was the obvious scapegoat. Although only very few City firms had actually lost money in the A.G.E. crash, most others thought it best to steer clear of any of the companies which had made up the group.

Now that I can see events in perspective, I marvel that at this point I didn't abandon hope. For I didn't. I don't remember even wondering what would happen if I failed. I was determined to succeed, and, like Queen Victoria on another occasion, so far as I was concerned the prospects of defeat did not exist.

Even when I made some headway with a few of the merchant bankers and other people I saw, I came up against a major obstacle which I just could not budge.

On the rare occasions when a backer talked of putting up money, his terms were that I should receive a fair salary, plus, maybe, a commission on profits above a certain level. And this was not my idea at all. I wanted a chance to make capital. To make cash—the stuff some lucky chaps get left them in wills.

But then, at last, I had a lucky break. Colonel Ruston, Chairman of Ruston & Hornsby Ltd., asked me to go and see him. Ruston & Hornsby was still then largely a family concern. Colonel Ruston himself had never worked in it. He had followed the traditional course of being called to the Bar. He might know little about engineering, but he was a shrewd man, with a trained, logical mind. He had heard of the difficulties I was in. He told me that his firm might be prepared to contribute towards buying these two companies off the Receiver, and to put me in as managing director on a salary plus a generous commission on profits. This though, would necessitate my companies' moving from Rochester to a fine modern works which Rustons owned at Grantham, in Lincoln-shire.

Rustons wanted at that time to dispose of this works so as to concentrate their manufacturing activities at Lincoln. Colonel Ruston had been told, he said, that the Aveling works at Rochester were not in the main, sufficiently modern for present-day require-ments.

I was pretty desperate by this time, but I told Colonel Ruston I would have to think his proposals over, and that my first reaction was that the difficulties were not insuperable but that I was definitely not prepared to go in just as managing director. I wanted a substantial block of shares, even if at the outset they weren't worth the paper they were printed on.

But I met Ruston's colleagues, and, in particular, his managing director, Mr. George Ruston Sharpley; his financial director, Mr. Pawlyn, a former Price Waterhouse man, and Mr. Percy, later Sir Percy, Lister, then a director of Rustons and also chairman of R. A. Lister & Company.

Rustons were not prepared to put up enough cash to buy up the two companies at Rochester, but they might put up perhaps £75,000 to help establish a company in their Grantham works. They would take payment in shares, and would probably require a majority of voting shares. If I could produce some scheme they were ready to examine it closely, but they hoped to avoid becom-ing part-owners of any more factories. They owned more than enough already.

Percy Lister and I quickly became firm friends and together we worked out a plan which, we hoped, would benefit all three parties, Rustons, myself, and the Lister Company. Percy Lister wanted our Rochester works for his friends, Winget Ltd., which made con-crete mixers. Winget Ltd. were on the lookout for larger premises. The plan we concocted was, very briefly, this:

Responsibility for finding the capital required to purchase the two Rochester companies off the Receiver would be left to me. If I succeeded in raising the cash, Rustons would lend the proposed new company £50,000 to cover the cost of moving plant, mach-inery, stock, stores, and work in progress from Rochester to

Grantham. We estimated that this sum would also enable us to build some offices at Grantham, as there were none. Rustons would lend us the money without security, but it would have to be repaid before the new company started paying dividends.

A £25,000 syndicate would be formed to own all the new company's Ordinary shares. Rustons would take up fifty-two per cent of these shares, and I would be given the rest. In other words, Rustons would be paying £13,000 for a controlling interest in the new venture, while my block of shares, nominal value £12,000 would be handed to me for nothing. This naturally was entirely my own idea. I had thought of a million penny shares or half a million because it didn't make a penny difference as at that time they were all valueless anyway.

The new company would agree to buy its engines, forgings, and castings from the Ruston group wherever possible, at cost plus ten per cent. I would be chairman and managing director, with the power to appoint one other director; two more would be nominated by Rustons.

This arrangement seemed to suit everybody if—and it was a large if—the new company could be successfully transplanted from Rochester to Grantham without more than temporary damage to output and not to much trading loss for a transitional period of say two years. Rustons were risking only £63,000 of their shareholders' money and if I succeeded they would have done an immensely profitable deal. My risk on the other hand was virtually 100 per cent, so I felt I must succeed—or go down fighting to the last.

As for me, of course, I stood to acquire £12,000 worth of "paper" shares which I might eventually make into something worth having—but not, I must stress, at the expense of the business itself or of those who had worked so loyally in it.

I had been to inspect the Ruston works at Grantham, accompanied by my own works manager from Rochester. The Grantham works comprised fine modern buildings and stood on a large site on the outskirts of the town. For any business hoping to expand in the future, here was a golden opportunity.

Avelings had their own foundry and forging shop at Rochester, but neither, as Colonel Ruston had been informed, was particularly modern. I was not especially happy about the agreement to order all our engines from Rustons, as I had been very friendly with the people who had supplied us at Rochester and we had worked closely together. But that couldn't be helped.

As far as Rustons were concerned, they had found someone to occupy works they did not want and employ the men who would otherwise become redundant when Rustons completed their move to Lincoln. And Rustons could well do with our custom. The tie-up whereby they were to supply all our engines would be immensely valuable to them, for the engine represents more than a quarter of the total cost of a diesel roller.

As for Percy Lister, Rustons made it very plain they did not wish to become part-owners of the Aveling works at Rochester, and Lister, as I have said, knew that Winget Ltd., an expanding Midlands firm manufacturing concrete mixers, were on the look-out for a new and much larger factory. Concrete mixers required engines, which Lister intended to provide. The Aveling works at Rochester were five or six times the size of Winget Ltd.'s existing works in the Midlands, and Lister, with my co-operation, wanted to do both himself and Winget Ltd. a good turn. Winget Ltd. have, during the succeeding thirty-five years, spent a great deal of money on our former Rochester works and both the buildings and layout are now vastly different to when we left it over thirty years ago.

I negotiated my provisional deal with Rustons by a simple exchange of letters between us, before proceeding to the main problem, which was of course to raise the money for the purchase of Aveling & Porter and Barford & Perkins from the Receiver. I had realized before meeting Colonel Ruston that my only remaining chance of raising money was one of the big joint stock banks: and I knew that, Rustons being one of the biggest concerns of its kind in the country, and held in the highest esteem everywhere, including the big banks, the deal I had provisionally fixed up with Colonel Ruston would stand me in good stead. In this I proved to be right.

The Ruston deal was of course entirely provisional until I succeeded in raising sufficient money. The strain was telling increasingly on our loyal staff at Rochester, and I was keener than ever to succeed. So the next step was to try to do a deal with the Receiver, and, if possible, get a three months' option.

I was confident that the grumpy Receiver would accept a low cash price. During the Great Depression a little ready cash went a long way. After some haggling I obtained a written three months' option at £100,000, paying £300 for it. I can't remember where this money came from. It certainly wasn't borrowed from Colonel Ruston as I didn't want his colleagues to know what desperate straits I was in.

After much thought I decided to approach Lloyds Bank to endeavour to borrow this £100,000. I had had dealings with them in the old days of A.G.E. Another reason for choosing Lloyds was that I didn't have a personal overdraft at any branch of that bank. At local branches of the other banks I did have overdrafts!

I was given an interview by Mr. R. A. Wilson, then a joint general manager at Lloyds' head office. Wilson was a most charming and courteous banker of the orthodox school: I had sent him my little brochure and he had studied it thoroughly: I suspected that he had also spoken to Mr. Charles Palmour on the telephone. According to the brochure the net assets of Aveling & Porter and Barford & Perkins together came to about £400,000. I handed Wilson copies of my provisional agreement with Rustons. He called in an assistant and we got straight down to brass tacks. I told him I wanted to borrow £150,000 on security of the above assets. He said the matter would receive consideration, and that he would phone me for a second interview.

I had seen him glancing at me, and he must have seen the strain and anxiety in my face. He told me very kindly that he would phone me back very soon; four days later I was in his office again. A few more questions, a few more replies taken down by a stenographer, and Wilson said that his colleagues had agreed to loan me the £150,000 as a debenture on our assets, and that, furthermore, the bank would consider extending me the normal banking facilities, including an unsecured overdraft, provided that the amount of the overdraft fluctuated – in other words, somehow I had to manage to be in credit occasionally, if only for a few days. Three days later I was to call again to sign the legal deed.

On the occasion of this third visit I was in an adjoining room with Wilson's assistant, studying the deed prior to signing it, when Wilson, the soul of courtesy, popped his head round the door and, after a friendly word or two, said,

"By the by, I don't think you mentioned the price on your option?"

"One hundred thousand pounds in cash," I said.

Wilson looked at me sternly, then asked me to come into his office.

"Let's get this absolutely clear," he said, "You are asking the bank to lend you £150,000 on the security of assets which you hold an option to purchase – with our money – for only £100,000. The deed you are to sign is personal, so the loan is also personal. It looks as if you're perfectly free to make £50,000 for yourself here and now, and possibly more later. You've explained to us, and given us figures to show that these two businesses are in a much less shaky position now than when A.G.E. crashed, which was over six months ago. Legally, you're now at liberty to sell out for much more than £100,000 and become a rich man on the deal. But I'm not actually worried about that. A successful banker is foremost a judge of men, a judge of character and capability. I *am* concerned, though, about the ethics of banking. I never heard before of a £150,000 loan secured on £100,000 worth of assets. The maximum loan should have been seventy per cent – say £70,000!"

He was silent. I answered.

"I was desperately afraid you were going to ask me that question before," I said. "Had you done so, I'd have told you at once that I'd got the option for £100,000. But you didn't ask me. You are lending me this money on £400,000 worth of assets, not on the price I am going to pay for those assets with your money. The extra £50,000 will immensely improve our financial position and, therefore, the security of your loan."

I had prepared this reply already as I had been expecting Wilson to ask me how much I'd arranged to pay for the option at our first interview.

Wilson then proceeded to give me a short lecture on the theory of banking. The money bankers lent to chaps like me, he said, was money belonging to their many thousands of depositors, to whom the bank stood in the position of Trusteeship. But I could see that his brow was clearing all the time and in the end he said:

"Anyway, a banker never goes back on his word and I shall not attempt to do so."

He looked at me in an old-fashioned way and roared with laughter. "I shall have to notify my colleagues of this," he went on, "and I can already hear their derisive laughter. I shall be the recipient of rude remarks to the effect that I'm so senile I've forgotten the basic principles of banking."

Then he was serious again. "And remember," he said, "that the bank has a letter from you saying that your company's going to make profits of £40,000 per annum when you're installed at Grantham. Your reputation is at stake. If you fail to make that profit, the bank has every moral and business right to start calling in its loan, or part of it."

To this I replied that as far as reputations were concerned, I didn't have one yet, but that I hoped to acquire one. I confirmed that I was confident I could make the profit required and told him how I appreciated the friendliness of his warning. I knew that he was warning me to live up to the promises I had made, or else. Then we both went back to his assistant's room and signed the deed.

Some years later Mr. R. A. Wilson became chief general manager of Lloyds Bank. He and his bank have remained my firm friends and supporters to this day. I saw and lunched with Wilson and his colleagues as often as was mutually convenient, until Wilson's retirement. And years after that, when I had reached the stage when I was invited to take luncheon with the directors of the bank, and even to sit next to the chairman, I would tell successive chairmen my story and enjoy their reactions, because the chairmen of most banks are not, of course, professional bankers but men of wisdom and achievement in wide international fields.

Now that I'd got the loan, and at last achieved something concrete, I was able to spend more time at Rochester, and talk to the managers I had appointed or re-appointed. And I began to get cold feet over the projected move. I worried about the cost of the move itself, about having to build new offices, about the effect the move might have on output, trading profits, and goodwill.

Many of our staff had lived at Rochester all their lives, and so had their fathers and grandfathers. Their relations and friends all lived there too, they had children at school there, they belonged to clubs and associations there. If these fine chaps had to starve anywhere, they'd prefer it to be at Rochester where they were known and loved. The Ruston £50,000 loan would be absorbed entirely in the cost of the move, etc. The windfall of the extra £50,000 from Lloyds Bank would be a wonderful help to our strained finances. But would all this upset prove too damaging to the new company? If we didn't move we'd be no worse off.

And our trading results might be affected more seriously than I had calculated, and for a longer time. There are only 168 hours in every week, as I have observed before, and my calculations might well be wrong.

There was nothing to prevent my calling off the deal with Rustons – or vice-versa. The provisional agreement had been arrived at on a friendly and general basis only, but I was confident that Colonel Ruston would not have let me down at this stage, and I felt an equal obligation to him. But I had to bear in mind that the successful launching of the new company meant a great deal to all the staff and to many of the weekly wage-earners of the factory. At all costs I must not let *them* down. I knew that they were hoping – perhaps they were praying – that I would succeed in restoring to them their security and self-confidence. These are things which mean so much to that huge slice of citizens who are neither at the top nor the bottom of business life. Nor of course did I want to let myself down – but that is something I have stressed enough already.

To Rustons, on the other hand, the whole scheme was a mere bagatelle. It represented only a small sliver of their activities. The most Rustons could lose would be part of £63,000, and there were opportunities in plenty elsewhere, at rock bottom prices, during those dark days of slump.

So I sought out Colonel Ruston and told him of my recent misgivings as to the possible consequences of the move to Grantham. Fine fellow that he was, he replied at once that he was quite prepared to call the whole thing off. Nothing irreparable had been done. A certain amount of time would have been wasted, but Rustons had spent much more time on other projects that had come to nothing. That was just business. No official announcement had been made; the staff at Rochester had heard nothing official from me. Since Rustons had incurred some professional costs, for accountancy, valuing, and surveying, Colonel Ruston felt that we should reimburse his company to the extent in due course.

Much heartened by the Colonel's kind attitude, I saw R. A. Wilson again and told him the position, mentioning Ruston's generous offer. Wilson listened, and again made a second appointment for three days later.

At our second talk Wilson began by saying there were only twenty-four hours to every day, including Sundays, so naturally I would not have had time to investigate all the possible consequences of a deal such as had provisionally been agreed with Rustons. But he said that the fact that Rustons were to be intimately connected with my new company had exerted some influence in my favour—but not unduly. Wilson said he felt he knew me fairly well now, and that I had made a good impression on his colleagues. I had in fact lunched with them in the room reserved for the joint general managers, and they had all questioned me for about twenty minutes afterwards. In sum, Wilson and his colleagues felt that if Rustons were now going to drop out, I must deposit £10,000 with the bank in cash, in proof of good faith. I have forgotten the actual words used, but Wilson's meaning was clear. He and his colleagues were not prepared to concede this point, and they felt that £10,000 was the lowest amount possible in the circumstances. If the Rustons deal went through, no such personal deposit would be necessary.

I looked at Wilson and he looked at me, for a long time. He had been so friendly that I had hinted to him that I was heavily in debt as a result of my long battle, on behalf of the shareholders of A.G.E. with Rowland and his co-directors. I was confident that the decision to ask me for a deposit had not been taken by Wilson alone, and that I had him to thank that the proposed guarantee was not perhaps £20,000 instead of £10,000. Wilson knew I hadn't got the money, and he guessed that I wasn't going to demean myself by trying to borrow it without security.

All this was passing through my mind as Wilson and I sat looking at each other.

This was my project and mine alone, and I knew I must stand or fall by my own exertions. So I told Wilson that I fully appreciated the bank's attitude but that I could not avail myself of this offer.

Over half of the three months' option I had bought from the Receiver had now expired. There was need for speed. Most of my friends hadn't got £10,000 or, if they had, they could not afford to risk it. I knew, by now, a number of the inherited rich, or had known them before I started to work a sixteen-hour day and a seven-day week. They would probably have thought I was asking for charity, which would have been highly embarrassing for them and for me too. So from that moment in Mr. Wilson's office I swept from my mind my notion of accepting Colonel Ruston's offer to release me from my provisional agreement, and I told him so. We would move to Grantham towards the end of 1933 and endeavour to take in our stride any snags that might arise.

If Rustons had faded out and we had stayed at Rochester all I now required was this £10,000 cash for the Lloyds Bank guarantee and I should have been sole owner of the joint company subject of course to its huge load of indebtedness. I would willingly have sold a half share for this £10,000 cash in 1933. Actually a buyer would not have done so badly because now his interest in Aveling-Barford Ltd. would be worth well over £2½ million.

A sum of £10,000 cash went a long way in 1933 during the world slump and even from 1937 inflation has been seven times. But allowing for all this, it would not have proved such a dusty investment.

As I have said already, I had given myself the other half of the shares for nothing, so it cannot be called an investment in the City sense of the word. I had merely invested myself, together with my moderate brain, my willpower, and my ambition.

It was to be a big move. About a thousand tons of plant machinery, stocks, and stores, together with all our staff above a certain age who had agreed to come, and about a hundred of our factory workers. It was the biggest move ever made by the old London and North Eastern Railway.

Preparations for it had continued to go forward, as I had not told anyone of my eleventh-hour hesitations and fears. Now I put on pressure to accelerate our plans and to provide housing accommodation at Grantham. Part of Rustons' plans to move their existing manufacture of heavy oil engines to Lincoln, together with staff and workers, meant that housing would be available for some of our people, so we naturally arranged for them to move first. I also persuaded Grantham town council to put up fifty new houses for allocation to our chaps from Rochester. No security of tenure could, however, be guaranteed.

At the same time there was a number of legal and business considerations to attend to. The two companies, although operating as one in the Aveling & Porter works at Rochester, remained two separate legal entities, Aveling & Porter and Barford &

Perkins. This state of affairs needed sorting out, and there were several courses open to me.

The first, and most obvious, course would be to put the two companies into a Receivership of my own choosing. In view of the huge load of much overdue bills from various suppliers that we were saddled with, this would be the right and proper thing to do. We could then form a new company to be called Aveling-Barford Ltd., and buy from the Receiver the assets, but not the liabilities, of the two former firms. Seeing that our liabilities were entirely due to the loans the two firms had been forced to make to A.G.E., the new management would be under no legal or moral obligation to discharge them. This was the course I should have taken, and it was by far the easiest. If we wished, we could retain the goodwill of our suppliers, who by now expected nothing, by putting the new company under a voluntary obligation to settle up to a total of, say, one-third of those overdue accounts over, say, two years, and after a moratorium of one year. This would be quite a simple operation, a routine matter for lawyers and accountants. The formation of a new company with appropriate capital structure would also be simple, and the only thing of any importance we stood to lose by this sort of arrangement would be any tax losses for income tax purposes. In this instance, anyway, that amount would be trivial as both companies had managed to show a profit in their audited accounts until the date of A.G.E.'s crash.

The second course was a variation on the first. We could liquidate Barford & Perkins and sell it to Aveling & Porter, leaving the legal structure of the latter untouched. Then we could approach our trade creditors and get them to accept a moratorium and writing-down of debts. Most of our suppliers had known all about the loans Rowland had demanded and would realize that the new management was in no way responsible.

There were plenty of companies in much the same position as we were, as a result of the slump, and I studied their attempts to deal with the situation. In many cases creditors were being asked to accept moratoria and writing down of debts, and professional advisers might well have represented to us that this course would suit us as well as the first.

The third course would also be the hardest and indeed the most unfair to all concerned in the new venture. This would be for us to sell Barford & Perkins to Aveling & Porter and continue to shoulder the entire burden of inherited debt. The sole advantage of this course was our honour, and of course that we might retain to the full the goodwill of our trade suppliers. And this was the course I adopted. I have never seemed capable of following the easier paths. And in point of fact we gained nothing as far as suppliers' goodwill was concerned. Our main suppliers knew the A.G.E. story from the beginning, and didn't expect payment in full, or anything like it. They had written off the member-companies' debts in their audited accounts directly A.G.E. went broke.

In many firms the debt-collecting department is quite separate from both the selling side, who visit their customers' works to obtain orders, and the manufacturing side, who deliver the goods unless they are told – by the financial department – to withhold delivery.

And memories in business are short. Individuals do not necessarily hold the same positions for any great number of years. Many of the travellers who visited our works to obtain orders, together with their sales management, had no idea whether Aveling-Barford had shouldered its two predecessors' debts or not. Within a couple of years at most all those overdue debts had simply been forgotten about.

The other former subsidiaries of A.G.E. who adopted either of the two courses I had rejected for Aveling-Barford had a far happier experience – financially – because Receivership relieved them of most of their load of debt (incurred because of Rowland of A.G.E.) and their goodwill and trading position suffered only slightly and temporarily.

And then, of course, the slump which had pulled all Britain down was still acute, so that bankruptcy, writing-down of capital, moratoria, and so on, were recurring at the rate of half a dozen a week among the bigger firms and at the rate of scores a week among smaller ones.

And so I made the huge mistake of accepting in full this crushing load of debt for the naive reason that it would greatly add to the goodwill of the new Aveling-Barford Ltd. I could not have been more wrong. But we got by.

Quite apart from the legal and financial problems we also had some heraldic difficulty in moving to Grantham!

As it was the earliest engineering works in the county of Kent, Aveling & Porter had been permitted to use as their trademark the proud crest of Kent, the Rampant Horse. When it became known that we were moving to Grantham, Kentish men and men of Kent became united in a determination to prevent the Kentish Horse leaving the county. I cannot remember which faction my father's old friend, the Earl of Guildford, headed, but he was one; and the then Lord Cornwallis was another, or perhaps the other. I was officially informed that every effort would be made to prevent me using this trademark anywhere else but in Kent.

This was a more serious matter than might appear. I was determined to preserve faithfully the name and history of Thomas Aveling, one of the great inventors of his day, and his trademark was closely associated with him and his work. I didn't want to lose it without a fight.

I am sure that the defenders of the Rampant Horse of Kent were thinking, quite rightly, of their ancient heritage, and in principle I agreed with them, but I did not seem able to get it across to the men I talked to that the continued use of what was to us our own emblem was vitally important to us, particularly as we were forming a new company and moving to a new locality.

So I went to the College of Heralds in Victoria Street, London, and, after some research, they verified that Aveling & Porter were in every way entitled to use the emblem in any locality. So all was well.

There was another aspect. The old engravings at the College of Heralds showed the Horse of Kent reared up as a fighting stallion exuding defiance at every pore, and pumping smoke out of its nostrils in a way that would have done credit to a dragon. In the course of time, however, the emblem had gradually become what looked like a fat, cosy mare, rearing up in fright at some children. So I commissioned Mr. Gilbert Bayes, then President of the Association of Sculptors to carve the defiant prancing stallion of hundreds of years before. We had the model cast in silver. It stands about two feet six inches high in the board room of our head office at Grantham.

Towards the end of 1933 Aveling-Barford Ltd. moved to Grantham. The move itself was executed very quickly indeed, which added to the cost of it, but proved a great success. My deal with Rustons was now confirmed and legalized, and I appointed, under the terms of the deal, another director, while Rustons appointed two more, making four in all. My nomination was my elder brother, Geoffrey, while Rustons appointed their managing director, Mr. Sharpley, and their financial director, Mr. Pawlyn.

So far as I could see immediately following the move, everything had gone off as well as could be expected, which meant the planning had been good. We had brought from Rochester a very large amount of work in progress, and materials and components were being delivered by our suppliers. For a fortnight I took my first real holiday in years.

I could now sit back and take stock of my position. Up to 1933, with the training and experience I had gained, I had unconsciously been preparing myself to start up on my own, and it was only from that year onward that I could reasonably hope I would be in a position to make money for myself.

I told Rustons' that I was going to pay myself a salary of £2,000 a year until the company was making adequate profits. I owned shares to the nominal value of £12,000, which represented forty-eight per cent of the total. We owed Rustons £50,000, which had been completely absorbed in the costs of the move from Rochester. But we still had £40,000 of the £50,000 Lloyds Bank had loaned me over and above the £100,000 needed to buy Aveling & Porter and Barford & Perkins from the Receiver.

Our troubles, of course, were not over. I had given Mr. Wilson my word that Aveling-Barford would begin to show profits of at least £30,000 after twelve months at Grantham, and I was sure that we would. But after we'd been at Grantham about six months half the key men we had moved from Rochester had failed to settle down and gone back again. I interviewed a number of them before they left, and their reasons were pretty much the same.

Rochester is close to London and our chaps could get quickly and cheaply up to town for first-class football matches, for cricket at Lord's and the Oval in summer. Or they could watch cricket at nearby Canterbury—Kentish Men and Men of Kent have always been strong supporters of cricket. And, of course, young men in search of feminine companionship had Chatham and other heavily-populated areas very close at hand. Their comings and goings were not observed by neighbours.

Grantham, on the other hand, was then a small, isolated country town. It took a couple of years or so before we really became part of it. Today all this is completely changed. We have been at Grantham for over thirty years and are the largest employers in the district.

Other minor problems helped to upset the speed with which we settled down at Grantham. The result of it all was that in our second year we made little or no profit, instead of the £40,000 I had promised.

Naturally I was summoned to the head office at Lloyds Bank. I gave my reasons for my failure to keep my word. Mr. R. A. Wilson said that his bank had decided to ask me to accept a quick investigation of our books by a London firm of accountants, Davie Parson & Company, before making any decisions. I accepted this proposal with alacrity and the accountants could not have done their quick survey more courteously. They were most careful to avoid anything which could have caused alarm and despondency among my small senior staff.

Within a week of their leaving I was again summoned to the bank's head office. Mr. Wilson began by saying that everything had been done as quickly as possible to spare me the strain of waiting. He went on to say that the auditors' report had been largely verbal and had contained absolutely nothing against me or my company. I had not misled the bank in any way, but our progress had been delayed by factors which I had not anticipated. The auditors felt that from now on we should trade at a profit. We had lost about £20,000 in total and Mr. Wilson wound up by saying that so that we should not be short of a working capital the bank would increase their loan to us from £150,000 to £180,000.

This gave us all a tremendous boost.

I showed Lloyds Bank our figures at regular intervals, and the bank realized we were quickly pulling ourselves out of the wood. Our trade creditors continued helpful, and so did the bank. Wilson went on twitting me about what he called my "leading him up the garden".

By early 1937, in spite of a nasty shock in 1935 which I will recount in the next chapter, it was clear we could now make a Public Issue of capital. I had a valuation made which showed a surplus of assets over liabilities of over £400,000. I decided to reform our capital structure into £160,000 in £1 Preference shares and £160,000 in 5s. Ordinary shares.

The next step was probably one of the greatest hurdles of the lot. Rustons held fifty-two per cent of our total shares, and I the remaining forty-eight per cent. To issue Preference shares alone would have been difficult, and I knew that I would have to sell quite a slice of my forty-eight per cent to pay off the debts I still owed. I knew also that I would have to sell at a price very much lower than I hoped to make the shares worth in a few years' time. But that was just the rub of the green and it couldn't be avoided. However, I didn't want to sell a single share more than was absolutely necessary, so I went to a great family friend of mine, and contemporary, who was on the Stock Exchange. His name was Lord North and he died during the Second World War. At the time he was a comparative junior in a small, but good, firm of brokers. To his everlasting credit, North said at once that this was not the sort of thing his firm could handle successfully. He reminded me that I knew, socially, Basil Bebb, one of the able partners whom the highly successful G. C. Hoare had collected round him in his firm, then named Cohen, Laming Hoare. North suggested that I should see Basil.

I did so, and Basil took me to see Hoare, then probably the greatest single figure on the London Stock Exchange. I told Hoare that my plan was to suggest to Rustons that they should sell half their fifty-two per cent holding at par. Kit Hoare could then place all our Preference shares and twenty-six per cent of our Ordinary. Hoare was, and still is, a fast worker, and this interview lasted about ten minutes.

By this arrangement Rustons would get £40,000 for shares that had cost them £6,500 only three years previously. This represented a profit of over 600 per cent. Furthermore I'd been told that Rustons had written down their £13,000 worth of shares in their books by half, so it was obvious that they were looking to the other advantages from my deal with them, and not expecting dividends or capital appreciation.

I should explain that Rustons did not in fact control Aveling-Barford in the way that perhaps they thought they did. With their knowledge and consent I had given both myself and my brother Geoffrey long-term service agreements, and since I was chairman of the board I had the casting vote. In the event of a difference of views, therefore, I controlled the board of directors, and the board of directors controlled the company.

As it happened, no such differences arose, because Mr. Sharpley and Mr. Pawlyn were the most charming of colleagues. When my new proposals were put before Rustons board I naturally absented myself, but I was called back in a few moments to be told that Rustons would be delighted to accept my offer if my negotiations with Kit Hoare bore fruit.

I then saw Kit Hoare again, and he said that the proposed operation now presented no difficulties whatsoever. It was in fact something of far lesser account than he was accustomed to handle, but he would do it.

Meanwhile I had asked my solicitors what the usual fee was for such an operation. They said that about £10,000 to £15,000 would be appropriate. I suggested to Hoare that as this was a small and, to him, unimportant operation, and as my company was still poor, a fee of £2,500 might be acceptable to his firm. Kit Hoare nearly exploded and one of his partners, who was present, looked deeply shocked. Hoare appeared very insulted at first but then his good sense of humour got the better of him.

"I am expecting Sir George May of the Prudential at any moment," he said, "and when he comes I shall of course have to break off our interview. I don't haggle with people, I am accustomed to stating my terms and to having them accepted. I am referring, naturally, to some of the largest and most important business concerns in the country."

Our interview was taking place in Hoare's London home and just as he finished this sentence the door opened and Sir George May was announced.

I had never met Sir George, afterwards Lord, May before, though, like everyone else, I had heard stories about how he had changed much of the investment policy of the Prudential. Though none of it was ever made public, Sir George was credited with having backed in the very early days concerns like Marks & Spencer and the Rootes Brothers. Mr. Hoare introduced us, and then continued.

"Young Barford here," he said, "is just leaving, but I've arranged to place £160,000 worth of his Preference shares and about £40,000 worth of his 5s. Ordinary, which is a quarter of the total, at a few pence above par. I'm putting the Prudential down for £10,000 worth of the Ordinary," he said. Then he turned to Basil Bebb. "Basil," he said, "please make a note of that and advise the Prudential in due course." Then to me again, "Goodbye, Barford. I hope we shall meet again soon."

I was told afterwards that the rest of my shares were all placed within an hour or two the next morning. Kit Hoare just allocated them himself to his clients and his clients accepted his advice.

Now we were really off the river bed and sailing on our own. Out of the £160,000 raised by the sale of our Preference shares we paid back Rustons' £50,000 loan and reduced our debts to trade creditors to a more normal figure.

Our dealings opened with small markings of Ordinary shares at about 5s. 6d. and the Preference shares went to a small premium, as anticipated by Kit Hoare.

Since the forming of the company some three and a half years previously the banks had held the major portion of my shares as security for my overdraft. I did not want to sell any shares as I hoped to make them worth a great deal more than 5s. 6d. within the next two or three years, but I felt there was no alternative. I just longed to see a bank passbook with my name on it, in the black instead of the red, so I sold, through Kit Hoare's firm, enough shares to bring me in £12,000 in cash.

Aveling-Barford was now completely independent for the first time. Our obligations to purchase engines, forgings, and castings from Rustons were scrapped, but we continued our purchases as free agents, buying at competitive prices.

As long as I and those members of my family to whom I had given shares retained the bulk of their holdings, I was in virtual control of the company.

CHAPTER THREE

NEARLY BANKRUPTED

In 1935 a blow fell which might well have bankrupted the new, still struggling company, which was, to put it mildly, very short of ready cash. The backbone of the business had for the past fifty years been steam rollers, but for a decade or more the diesel-engined roller had been making rapid progress, particularly abroad. After much thought, I had decided in 1933 to lay out and equip the Grantham works solely for the manufacture of diesel-engined machines.

In the 1935 Budget proposals came a heavy tax on diesel oil used for certain general purposes which would automatically include the comparatively small road-roller industry. I realized at once that this would throw the home trade right back on to steam rollers. To build diesel rollers solely for export would be impossible. We needed our home trade, although it amounted to only twenty-five per cent of the total, even if only as a testing ground for new models. The outlook was black and the prospect of bankruptcy reared its ugly head – yet again.

So I decided to make an all-out effort to get road-rollers excluded from the new tax. For two months I worked night and day, writing, lobbying, talking. My efforts were regarded as a joke throughout our section of the engineering industry. How could one man expect to get an alteration made in the Budget, just to suit his own company? Moreover, I was the largest holder of what were still "paper" shares. If the Treasury gave way in one instance, where would it end – what a precedent would be set! And for the big as well as the small!

After many exhausting interviews with the Board of Trade and with Treasury officials, some of whom were just uninterested and bored, gradually working up the line, I knew that I had made a friend or two. I know that some of these languid officials just did not want to take any sort of responsibility. They were all right as they were, as part of the Establishment. So "courtesy and do nothing" was the correct procedure, "pass the buck" the right motto. Then nobody got into trouble. Those who had already received their "K" would risk no criticism and those near to receiving it didn't wish to put a foot wrong. I found that not all civil servants were firmly stuck in the groove, but that those who were not were sadly in a minority, particularly near the top. So I realized that my case depended on someone very high up believing in the necessity of exports. Someone who recognized the old maxim of well-established manufacturers – "Export trade must be based on a sound home demand, even though it's smaller."

I learned that this man was Mr. Neville Chamberlain, then Chancellor of the Exchequer, and he knew it because his forbears had been steeped in it, just as had the Avelings and the Barfords.

But how did a young man like me get the personal ear of the Chancellor himself?

Eventually Mr. Chamberlain sent for me. He told me that he had looked at the papers concerning the case and that he realized the huge efforts I had made. He told me, in front of the assembled high officials and his parliamentary aides, that he would accept the amendment I proposed, which meant altering just five or six words to exclude road rollers – and nothing else – from the appropriate clause in his Budget.

And in due course I sat in the Distinguished Strangers' Gallery – for the first, but by no means the last, time – and heard Captain Charles Waterhouse put the amendment, and Mr. Neville Chamberlain accept it.

Other, but lesser blows came later. These included an Excess Profits Tax, introduced some time before the war, which favoured most heavily and unfairly the old, well-established concerns, including banks, insurance companies, and almost everything else in the City, at the expense of the younger, rapidly-growing businesses like ours.

This stupidity (a stronger word is appropriate) took 1935, two years before Munich, as a basis year. But we had expanded three times since this basis year! So our net available profits so urgently required to bring back the new company to the glory of its two predecessors twenty years previously was stolen by government decree. And this crazy iniquity continued until about 1945.

To recap, we start in 1934, the basic year is 1935 and this continues in successive acts until 1945. And in the House of Commons our legislators claimed that they were being equitable.

Retained profits to pay for the most modern machinery, to develop projects and to provide more cash to carry them out together with paying their losses on the mistakes – these are the lifeblood of industry.

I deal with this matter elsewhere.

But I faced up to this blow realistically. It was, to say the least, ill-considered legislation at a time when the country had at last started to arm and when every right-minded citizen wished to avoid any recurrence of what had happened during the First World War, when profiteering had apparently been rampant.

Being among the many veterans of the First World War who feared before Munich that conflict was inevitable, I was pleased to receive a personal request from Mr. Duff Cooper, who knew me, suggesting that Aveling-Barford be numbered amongst a list of concerns ready to "educate" themselves in the business of making armaments by taking on a limited amount of suitable work without fuss or publicity.

When the international situation worsened, Aveling-Barford was asked to drop all peacetime manufacture and go hell for leather on Bren gun carriers, increasing output as much as possible.

By this time Aveling-Barford was fully experienced in this sort of work, but more floor-space and more machinery were vitally urgent. I remembered well my own experience in 1916, as a youth of eighteen. My battery, and every other in the vicinity, were rationed to two shells per gun per day while the Germans blasted our positions to blazes all day and every day.

So again I made up my own mind. It took but a day or two to discover that the machinery for obtaining official approval for a government-financed shadow factory, or for the usual fifty per cent government grant to a firm's own expansions, would take months of planning, of suggested amendments, and so on *ad infinitum*. I cut through it all and borrowed the money from Lloyds Bank so that we could build our own extensions. Because of all the red tape, not a penny was received by my firm for its prompt action in altering the factory and in purchasing much additional machinery before the outbreak of the war.

But once the war started the country gained greatly from our unilateral action. No less than forty per cent of all carriers that went to France with our ill-fated Expeditionary Force under Lord Gort had been manufactured by Aveling-Barford. Between them Nuffield, Thorneycroft, and the smaller Sentinel company had manufactured the remaining sixty per cent — having waited, quite properly, for official orders before embarking upon manufacture.

It is sad to think that, if war had not broken out, much of our expenditure upon materials and wages could well have been repudiated by officialdom.

Not a penny did we ever get from the Government, because our detailed plans for extending and equipping the factory were not "Previously officially approved".

I was, in fact, very unpopular with the top brass, and became even more so at the end of 1942.

I had been campaigning all along, since 1937, that the supremely important thing was to get every factory in the country in full production. To my mind it was of minor importance that there existed on paper, or in the early experimental stage, improved designs. These could be incorporated at a later stage. For the time being nothing should be allowed to impede maximum production. After all, hundreds of millions of pounds had been spent in the six years before the war; and a large whack of that had been solely devoted to the designing, experimenting with, and testing of all the pieces of mechanical equipment needed in battle.

Officialdom, however, whether in uniform or not, seemed to be for ever bringing production in many factories to a standstill in order to introduce improvements and modifications. This was all very well in 1936 to 1938, but when war actually broke out my oft-repeated motto was "Any tank is better than no tank, any armoured vehicle better than no armoured vehicle, and any machine gun carrier better than no machine gun carrier".

No, I was not popular. And I dubbed certain very highly-placed experts "The Crazy Gang", which unfortunately leaked out, reaching the ears of the Biggest Wig of them all.

Soon after the end of the Phoney War I suggested that the War Office should take all the old First World War tanks from village squares and war memorials. New engines, guns, and whatever else might be necessary could easily be fitted, and the tanks overhauled and sent to war again.

This was a serious suggestion, but it was not taken as such, and I was shouted down. Even Lord Beaverbrook was displeased. As a matter of fact I had done limited research on the matter, the results of which were very satisfactory. Feeling, as I did, right from the rise to power of Hitler and Mussolini, that in a Second World War our fighting troops would be, comparatively speaking, just as ill-equipped vis-à-vis their enemies as their fathers had been in 1914, I had discovered that many of these tanks on war memorials were complete down to the last detail. The moving parts had even been greased, presumably before the machines left their army workshops to be placed in position on village squares.

The net result of it all was that Lord Beaverbrook took me from the Hotel Cecil, then his main headquarters, to Number Ten Downing Street, in the rather old-fashioned Rolls he used during the war, and I entered the Cabinet Room for the first and only time of my life. My dismissal and the parting handshakes — there was only Churchill, Beaverbrook, and myself — took only a minute or so.

Churchill was certainly angry over my apparent insubordination to the Big Wigs, but his parting shot made me laugh: "And not even a K for you."

CHAPTER FOUR

MECHANIZING THE INFANTRY

ONE of the things I had thought over as I lay in hospital after the First World War was how very tired physically the average soldier was during battle before he came even in sight of a German. This is, of course, exactly the opposite to what it should be. In Roman times a gladiator entered the arena in the very pink of condition. The Roman soldier used to march along with his own little group of camp followers to carry his heavy leather armour, his helmet, his shield, and his weapons. He himself was walking along in his underpants (as it were) as fresh as a daisy. By 1914, all these years later, we had reached exactly the opposite where the soldier was loaded up by his heavy uniform, his rolled waterproof ground sheet, gas mask, cooking utensils, iron rations, rifle, ammunition, and all the other paraphernalia he was forced to carry slung about him, weighing in all I think more than sixty pounds.

Seeing that the commanding officers usually did not know exactly at what point they would first make contact with the enemy, a number of miles was usually covered on foot before engaging the Germans. My point was that before they fired their first shot in anger, our chaps were often two-thirds worn out physically.

One evening at the beginning of 1937 or thereabouts an idea occurred to me. This is how it happened.

The Café de Paris was then one of London's leading dining places. The cabaret turn was a chap who cycled onto the empty dance floor on a complete bicycle and then proceeded to take off piece after piece – handle-bars, seat, one part of the frame, and then another, and then one wheel – until finally he was cycling upon one wheel only. The turn has been copied many times since.

It was then that the idea hit me. In self-defence I must point out that my mind was very much obsessed with military matters as it was only a few weeks previously that Churchill had first contacted me, as I shall tell later, and asked me to tell him what I knew, in my limited sphere, of our unpreparedness for war.

I am afraid I bored my beautiful companion by thinking aloud.

My idea, though, was quite simple. It was to have designed a very light-weight, low-built motor cycle, to be built by the tens of thousands, with completely interchangeable parts and each part, including the engine, to be capable of being snapped out or in, in a second or two. In other words, if an engine failed or a tyre burst, the rider could snap out the engine or the wheel and snap in another. In addition the whole machine would be so designed as to allow for everything the soldier had to carry, except his uniform and his boots, to be snapped on to the frame and still leave room for the soldier himself to take a ride if the ground was suitable.

The tiny engine of perhaps one horse-power would be very low-geared with two speeds, one a normal walking pace and the other twice as fast. Over ordinary grassland in low gear a soldier would be able to walk along beside the machine, relieved of some sixty pounds of weight, and get himself pulled along. There was also to be a shield so that if he was unexpectedly fired upon by the enemy he could drop the cycle to the ground, snap up the shield, and lie behind it while loading his rifle. The whole machine to be about one-third the weight of the standard W.D. motor cycle and much smaller frame and wheels.

My idea was that these little machines should be produced in such large quantities and with such an enormous supply of spares as to be completely expendable in whole or in part. I thought that the great high troop transport lorries should be capable of carrying a dozen and a half of my machines tucked away underneath.

At this time Aveling-Barford had been in production for only three years, but we employed in our Glasgow depot two ingenious craftsmen, both named Henderson, who had already been marked down as enjoying a bit of inventing. These men were also keen cyclists. So I had them both down for a couple of days to explain my ideas and talk things over with them. We pulled in a local colonel whose battalion was training in the area, and borrowed from him one of everything a soldier had to carry. The Hendersons took everything back with them to Glasgow, and within a fortnight had come to the conclusion that the whole idea was not only feasible but, indeed, dead easy so far as producing the little machine itself was concerned. They immediately proceeded to build a mock-up.

This taught us a great deal and then the brothers Henderson built two trial machines. The performance of these was all that we had anticipated and I was delighted that my original idea was proved practicable.

Then I went to the top brass in London with written descriptions, photographs, and explained my ideas. I made it plain at the outset that the whole scheme was not of the slightest business interest to Aveling-Barford. Our manufacturing facilities were entirely unsuitable for such a light repetition job, but that these little machines of course could be very simply and easily produced in great quantities by cycle and motor cycle manufacturers plus the manufacturers of very small petrol engines of which there were several very efficient ones. I said that this was a personal idea of my own which I had carried just far enough to show that it was practicable and that I would now be pleased to hand it over to the War Office gratis, though if the idea were further developed and employed I should like my name to be associated with it. I was most disappointed with the reactions I received at each of the several interviews that I had, usually with different officials. Officialdom is basically averse to any fresh or novel ideas from an outsider. They could not get it through their heads that this was not just another form of motor cycle to be used by a few men in each battalion, whereas I meant it to be a piece of standard equipment for every foot soldier. Being so light and produced in such quantities it could be abandoned in battle at any time. They kept reiterating that the infantry did not carry one ounce more than was necessary. I did not question this in any way. I was confining myself to a small machine that would *inter alia* do the carrying for him.

They also kept reiterating that Army motor cycles were getting heavier, not lighter. I went to see these military motor cycles being tested which included riding them over sheer drops of more than six feet so no wonder the wheels, tyres, frames, etc. were being made heavier and heavier. I could not get them to appreciate that I was not talking about their existing motor cycles at all or even thinking of supplanting them. I was suggesting an extra piece of equipment which would have all the advantages to the ordinary foot soldier that I have mentioned above.

One man did take a different view. He was Major Le Q. Martell, later to be famous as one of the most brilliant technicians on our side. He commanded an armoured division, the first I think, and ended up as Lieut.-General Sir Giffard Le Q. Martell.

The owner of Loch Lomond, or part of it, had kindly allowed the Henderson brothers to use the lakeside as a testing ground. Martell accompanied me to Loch Lomond and he agreed with me that we had proved that the idea was entirely practicable though, of course, the Henderson machines were just mock-ups and, if the idea was adopted by the War Office, the machines would have to be designed for mass production throughout.

But the scheme was never adopted so that my idea of mechanizing the ordinary soldier was still-born. Martell however pushed it through that I should receive a government grant of £500 which I gave to charity. But my idea was right and should be adopted today.

It was most fortunate for the armed forces and Britain as a whole that so many executive heads of engineering groups in 1936/9 were themselves veterans of the First World War and they already despised officialdom as heartily as I did.

Our particular sphere was confined to armoured vehicles that moved upon tracks, and the like, but it was clear the situation was not much different in every other field featuring equipment needed in war by fighting men. Some of us took the bit between the teeth, and went on urging our chaps to greater output whether we had received official orders or priorities, or not. And the emphasis is on the "not". The usual procedure was as follows; about half a dozen high officials would tell you as managing director that you were to make a certain number of, let us say, machine-gun carriers. Another six chaps would then say no, you were not to, as they were considering "directing" your company to make something else, like a light tank. Then another bunch of chaps would say that big improvements in the design of machine-gun carriers were on the way, so we should hold up production for a month or two until the new, improved designs were available.

So far as I remember we started manufacture of Lloyd Carriers eighteen months before we received the great bundle of documents which compromised the official order. Captain Vivian

Lloyd, a noted inventor, was and remains my friend, and I instructed my able works manager to go ahead as I was ignoring the official constipation in issuing their bumph.

The manufacturers who listened to all this top brass found themselves actually short of work in the most desperate phases of the war.

This really was one of the main reasons for shortages of fighting equipment both before and during the war. Officialdom breeds delay and lack of decision.

Having already touched on the machine-gun carriers affair, perhaps I might relate what happened in more detail.

In the autumn of 1936 Mr. Duff Cooper, then Secretary for War and an acquaintance of mine, asked me to go and see him. In a five-minute talk he explained that he was looking for a number of medium-sized firms not previously connected with armaments which might be prepared to educate themselves in suitable armaments production on a small scale, so that production could be swiftly augmented in the event of increased world tension. Obviously the Government did not wish to attract great publicity to this scheme, so firms not situated in densely populated areas were desirable. Duff Cooper's wife's ancestral home, Belvoir Castle, was only four miles from Grantham, and he had been round our works with me. He felt that Aveling-Barford might be suitable. His staff had agreed, and had suggested that we start educating ourselves in the manufacture of machine-gun carriers. Would I like to consider the matter and then talk it over with a senior member of his staff?

I replied that there was no necessity for consideration, and passed straight away into another room to hear further details. The upshot was that I was given, there and then, a verbal order to manufacture twenty-five machine-gun carriers in time for the summer (1937) manoeuvres of the Brigade of Guards, then about nine or ten months off. I said, of course, that to meet this schedule the War Office would have to move a great deal more swiftly than I had ever known it to do before. We should need the drawings immediately and we should subsequently need assistance in getting materials and components in double quick time. There were no government priorities at the time, but none were needed as almost every big concern was managed by men who had fought the Germans face to face in the First World War and who were already putting their own interpretation on Germany's present re-armament. My remark about the War Office's traditional lack of speed was resented by the group of chairborne officers to whom I was talking, but I didn't mind as I had meant it to be. I felt they needed a bit of shaking up or it would be many weeks, or even months, before we received the drawings necessary to start work on the carriers.

I proved more right – for once – than I could possibly have imagined. For weeks and weeks nothing happened whatsoever. No letter confirming our interview, no official order, nobody came near Grantham, and, worst of all, no drawings. After patiently waiting for about six weeks I telephoned and called by appointment on one or two of those high-ranking officers. They expressed the greatest surprise that I had heard nothing. I should have mentioned that at our first interview they said that the drawings were all ready and would be sent down in a few days. You should have received the drawings weeks ago, they said. An official order always took a little time, but we should have had a written letter of authority. They would look into it without a moment's delay.

Whereupon the whole exercise was repeated, the weeks of patient waiting, the second interview, the same expression of shock and amazement.

After that I gave up. Apparently they didn't want us to make the gun carriers and had found others more suitable. I had not forgotten the First World War and our ration of two shells per day, so sincerely hoped this was so.

But a few months later there arrived at Grantham, quite unexpectedly, two carloads, one containing officers from the Brigade of Guards and the other containing top War Office officials. Naturally they were all in civilian clothes, but they explained who they were and said they had come in the hope of seeing some of their carriers on test. Failing which, they imagined that at any rate they could see them in an advanced stage of construction, seeing that their summer manoeuvres were now less than three months off.

I was in London that day, but my colleagues knew the whole story and had to tell them that not a single working drawing had ever been received and that as a result nothing had been done. We hadn't even been able to order the raw materials. The only thing we had received, I think, was a letter of authority to build the carriers "to the specifications and drawing already in your possession". This letter went on to say that in the interest of the general public the whole order would be subject to contract, that we made only reasonable returns on capital employed, and that we agreed to make all our books and accounts available to the Costing Department of the Ministry.

This was standard procedure and would certainly have been in the interest of the general public had it been promptly and properly applied.

The tragic thing was that the Ministry was apparently relying on Aveling-Barford and two other firms to educate themselves in the manufacture of machine-gun carriers, yet after nine months no drawings had been delivered upon which we could at least make a start. If only we had been sent the drawings I would not have bothered about an official contract, as I already knew that a contract took a dozen officials several months to draw up. And I already knew enough of our total unpreparedness for war to appal me.

I had the entrée, both personal and official, to factories and I went round them with a couple of my own technical and production chaps and I was further appalled – hideously appalled – at what I saw for myself in this limited sphere of tanks and armoured vehicles. As I left my small office in Aldwych House I would look at all the younger chaps hurrying home after a good day's work. Had they begun to realize that they were destined to be cannon fodder, just as their valiant fathers had been twenty-five years before?

I started to raise merry hell, and Mr. Duff Cooper himself was among those highly incensed at my story. I told Duff Cooper who, as War Minister, had enlisted me on the original Tank Committee (afterwards redivided, renamed, and enlarged into half a dozen committees, each of which was carefully enmeshed in lovely new red tape), that I was going to see Neville Chamberlain direct. As I have already related, he had been most helpful to me over the fuel tax in the Budget of 1935, and he had sent people to see me on export matters several times, so to a very limited extent, he was accessible to me when he became Prime Minister.

I prayed an official interview and, after a Cabinet meeting, he let me blow my top for ten minutes in front of him, half a dozen ministers, and a covey of permanent officials. My theme was that in spite of the £5,000 million Armament Programme I was convinced and horrified that the First World War would repeat itself in our unpreparedness. Young Barford's views upon our appalling lack of armaments in spite of all the expenditure and entirely contrary to ministerial speeches, got round in a limited circle.

At this time Duff Cooper mentioned my name to Winston Churchill and suggested that we might meet. If I wished it, Duff would arrange it at a mutually convenient time and place.

Churchill was the man who only a few years later was to become the virtual Dictator of England. But at the time it must be remembered that he was still in "outer darkness". Though Winston Churchill, who had attained Cabinet rank at such an early age, was a fine and forceful orator, a man who filled the House of Commons whenever he spoke, he was not in the Government and it must have looked to him, as well as to everybody else, that he would never be in a Cabinet again. But his influence with the public was large. His speeches were prominently reported and commented on. He had a large number of well-wishers and supporters up and down the country.

I saw Churchill, and he told me that he was worried about the rate of our re-armament and our general unpreparedness for possible hostilities. If satisfactory facts and figures could be given to the public, through Parliament, showing our progress, if even the spies of other countries could report to their masters that our re-armament programme was going well, then Britain and the rest of the world could play a powerful part in preserving peace.

Churchill felt that the replies in the House of Commons were too vague, and that the necessity for secrecy was overdone. He needed ammunition for an attack on the whole matter in the House, so that both Parliament and the public should know whether, indeed, the position was satisfactory.

So I told him my story of the machine-gun carriers. He listened intently. I told him of other facts that had come to my knowledge together with names and figures. I gave him the whole works and a secretary took down all I said. I handed him a memo I had prepared.

He thanked me warmly.

Then—did I mind risking unpopularity by finding out more concrete facts within my own sphere which included light and medium tanks or other facts outside my sphere?

I replied that, in my view, the general public together with almost all the House of Commons were being lulled into a totally false sense of security so far as armaments were concerned, and that I would regard it as my duty to find out what more I could—adhering to facts and figures and not mere hearsay.

It was the first of several interviews and talking sessions up to the outbreak of war.

I now revert to Aveling-Barford and the machine-gun carriers. Eventually with me hammering at the top and my chaps at Grantham hammering all down the line, the drawings began to arrive.

Within an hour of the first machine moving under its own power on our road roller testing ground, we had it photographed and I rushed up to London with half a dozen copies (still damp) in my business case. I shot them round the desks of the various officers in the War Office.

Then we had a second verbal order, though we still of course hadn't had the contract for the first, and now we really got going, ignoring the War Office Contracts and Costing Department, and everybody else. Things were pretty tense internationally by now and neither my colleagues nor myself were going to be held back by anyone if we could help it.

And so it was that eighteen months or so later, at Dunkirk, General Lord Gort had practically no tanks at all but quite a number of machine-gun carriers, over a third of which were built by Aveling-Barford.

It would have been a funny business if it wasn't so tragic.

CHAPTER FIVE

I ATTEMPT THE IMPOSSIBLE

GRANTHAM Productions, an armaments company, sprang into life about the outset of the war manufacturing principally a 20 mm quick-firing gun called the Hispano Cannon. Government money was introduced on a large scale and Grantham received great publicity, official visits from lesser royalty and top brass, and telegrams for public consumption praising this particular contribution to the war effort. But the existing factories in Grantham were equally engaged upon fighting armaments and this newest addition, lacking skilled machinists, etc., was accused locally of attracting these key men by offering wages well above the prevailing levels – maybe deliberately, maybe not. Since all armament production was on a cost-plus basis (a stultifying product of mass bureaucracy) the only loser in such a competition was the national purse.

Not unnaturally, my factory management felt that chaps who had learned their skills with us, and who were happy with us, should not be induced elsewhere. Other established local firms felt the same.

Feelings ran alarmingly high in the smallish town of Grantham so I went to see Beaverbrook and received a coolish though friendly reception. He said, "Money doesn't matter at this stage of the war. These factories are 100 per cent government property. So you plan to take them over, when the time comes. I'll mark the papers about them."

In the middle of the war the Auditor General bobbed up and expressed concern, so Churchill or Beaverbrook put Lord Bennet of Canada and Lord Ashfield on the board of the company.

After the war ended, on Beaverbrook's wartime advice I made my official application for these government-owned factories on the terms which had then become standard.

Three successive presidents of the Board of trade, Dr. Hugh

Dalton, Mr. Oliver Lyttelton, and Sir Stafford Cripps, allocated these factories to Aveling-Barford. Yet, at the last moment, by the personal direction of Sir Stafford Cripps, the factories were re-allocated to a group including Mr. Denis Kendall, M.P. for the production of a £100 "People's Car".

I went to see Sir Stafford Cripps by appointment and put my case in the course of a ten minute purposely unwritten statement. I also reminded him that the first time I had met him, in that same President of the Board of Trade's room, I had told him, in front of his assembled advisers and aides, that in my view the late Henry Ford, Lord Nuffield, and the Rootes Brothers all rolled into one could not build a £100 car in a factory of that size and with only £1 million capital. (Subsequently, and as I had predicted, less than a year after its start, the much publicized "People's Car" venture went bankrupt.)

Cripps seemed very sympathetic, but five weeks later sent one of his aides to tell me that his existing decision must stand. He did not want to see me again, but somehow I managed to get into the President's room at the House of Commons a fortnight later. I met with a chilly reception.

This surprised me, for Sir Stafford had always been most help-ful to me. The letter reproduced in this chapter was a kindly and sympathetic gesture to me. Why was he now using every endeav-our to bottle me up and push me off the scene entirely? And why was he belittling the whole matter as something trivial and unimportant?

Meanwhile frequent articles about the "People's Car" project were appearing in the national press, and it was announced that an Indian potentate, the Maharajah of Navagwana, had agreed to put a million pounds into the company. The Maharajah had come to England for the purpose, and was staying at the Savoy Hotel – but he wasn't giving any interviews to the press.

It seems, however, that Mr. John Hall of the *Daily Mail* must have been sleeping on a door-mat in the hotel corridor, for various articles about the Maharajah appeared in the *Daily Mail* under his name. It was thus that I learned that a special allocation of steel had been awarded to the Maharajah and his associates in the "People's Car" venture.

Quite a remarkable coincidence now occurred. Aveling-Barford were clients of Foster Turner Ltd., the City advertising agents, and one of the principals of this firm, Edward Clifford-Turner, was and is a good friend of mine. I had told him casually that Aveling-Barford was applying for the Grantham factories, but naturally not a thing more. Edward Clifford-Turner rang me up one day on business and at the end happened to mention that his partner, Foster, acted as equerry to the Maharajah of Navagwana when he visited England.

I already knew that Foster was one of the four Foster brothers, famous in the cricketing world. He also mentioned that the Maharajah was none other than the nephew and heir of the great Ranjitsinghi, of great cricketing fame in his day.

This made me leap with excitement because Ranji had been a lifelong friend of my cricketing uncles, the late W. R. Moon and L. J. Moon. I myself had first known Ranji when I was nine or ten years old, as Ranji was often at W. R. Moon's home at 69 Avenue Road, Regent's Park. Ranji admired W. R. Moon immensely. Bill Moon's father, senior partner of their family firm of solicitors, several generations old, called Moon, Gilks, and Moon, had died early and suddenly, when Bill, aged seventeen, was still at Westminster School. For financial reasons, it became necessary for Bill to qualify as a solicitor as quickly as possible. He was eldest of three boys and four girls. He set to, and became a solicitor, but he didn't give up his athletic activities. At Westminster he was an outstanding athlete. He had already been marked down for higher things, namely the possibility of playing soccer for England, but it was agreed by all, except young Bill Moon himself, that he would have to give up entirely such a glittering prospect, as, training to become a solicitor, he would never have any time to practise, coaching, or training, except for about three hours on Saturday afternoons. He was cramming every evening, seven days a week. However, two years later, or maybe three, this overworked young man was taking a horse-bus to the ground to captain England at soccer.

Bill was one of the most famous of the Corinthians. The Corinthian Club could and did take on teams, professionals, and amateurs, chosen from every footballer in England who was not a member of the club itself. A couple of years or so ago, the *Sunday Telegraph* published a fine article on the history of the Corinthians and their astounding soccer successes against the professionals. There was one illustration only – a photograph of W. R. Moon.

In the summer Bill played cricket, and he preferred the Hampstead Cricket Club, I think, to the M.C.C. In those days, too, Hampstead C.C. could put teams into the field that took a lot of beating at Lord's, the Oval, or anywhere else.

But it was L. J. Moon, who was killed in the First World War, who was perhaps Ranji's greatest friend, and the two of them behaved like schoolboys together. L. J. Moon was a double – if not a triple – Blue at Cambridge, was capped by England for both cricket and soccer, and spent the first thirty years of his life playing those two games, and indulging in other sporting activities such as big game shooting with Ranji, who, when he went on tour to India, entertained him in royal state.

When visiting England, Ranji often avoided staying in hotels. Instead he rented houses of a size appropriate to his rank in India. Now and again, however, he would spend a night or two on one of the couches in the "club-room" at my uncle's home. Ranji was the most charming and friendliest of chaps, even to small boys who badgered him for twenty or more autographs which they promptly sold off at school, but he was always conscious of his royal status in India and while officially in England felt obliged to stay at the Savoy Hotel in appropriate splendour, complete with entourage.

My uncle toured South Africa and Australia as well as India, with as many Test teams as he could afford.

He was killed at Gallipoli with the Brigade of Guards in the First World War. How he passed his medical as a temporary soldier, nobody knew, because L. J. Moon had smashed one knee badly at soccer and in spite of the appliances he wore the cartilage was always slipping out of place. This apparently happened several times at Gallipoli, and once too often. His company was in retreat, the cartilage slipped, and he lay helpless on the ground until the Turks came up and bayoneted him.

I have talked about my two uncles at some length because I realized as soon as Edward Clifford-Turner rang off that this gave me a very strong lever to meet the Maharajah. After a day's careful thought, I decided to tell Edward Clifford-Turner the whole story, in order to enlist his support, and have his partner, Foster, whom

I knew but slightly, arrange a private meeting between me and the Maharajah. I knew I could trust Clifford-Turner implicitly but he was not to say anything to Foster except that I was the nephew of the Maharajah's uncle's greatest friend, and that Ranji had given me a tête-à-tête luncheon only three weeks before he died.

By this time, Foster had been told some more, and had guessed more still, so I hatched a little plot. The plot was that I should ask Lord Woolton and Lord Kemsley to take luncheon alone together at Claridges. Foster, Clifford-Turner, and I would be at an adjoining table. Clifford-Turner and I would then talk loudly to Foster, who was not in on the plot, about the £100,000 worth of shares that the Maharajah – for so I had learned – had to give certain persons of influence. We would embellish this story with loud exclamations as to how shocked and horrified Ranji would have been at such bribery and corruption in high places. The two of us practised at least twice beforehand and we had at least half a dozen different questions and answers ready to bring out at any given point. All we wanted was for Woolton or Gomer Kemsley to hear Foster say something, it didn't matter what, which clearly showed that he knew all about this £100,000 and where it had gone to. If Foster did not talk loud enough, we had arranged to shout back his own answer or substitute an answer to the same effect back at him, so as to make him at least nod in the affirmative. We each had a stiff card in our pocket reminding us of suitable cues, and we didn't think the plot could possibly fail. But it did.

I realized afterwards that we were mere boobs and amateurs at this sort of thing. Foster was no fool, and he was also Ted Clifford-Turner's partner in business, so knew him intimately. In our eagerness, I think we mentioned the Grantham factories too soon. Foster wanted to talk to me about my uncle and Ranji and how often they had played in the same match, sometimes in the same team and sometimes not. When we mentioned the Grantham factories he said right out that this was the one subject he preferred not to discuss, but we went on, raising our voices whenever we mentioned that £100,000 bribe. Foster was thinking hard, I am sure. He knew all about it, of course, and now he was learning that we knew too. Furthermore, he was intensely loyal to his

Maharajah, the nephew of his old pal Ranji. He knew all about an interview between Woolton and the Maharajah, and had probably been present at it. He looked a bit angry at being set upon like this by two chaps, one of whom was his partner. He glanced around as if looking for a means of escape and there, sitting at the next table and gazing hard at him, was a face which he recognized as being that of Lord Woolton. He looked further but Gomer Kemsley had snatched up the large menu and was hiding behind it. Mr. Charles, the great maître d'hôtel, was hovering near these two distinguished lunchers at that moment. I expect he wondered what Lord Kemsley was doing, looking at a menu when he was half way through luncheon. I don't know what he said, but, with a bow, he deftly removed the menu from Lord Kemsley's hand, and Foster immediately recognized that face too. The game was up. Their Lordships gave me one or two angry glances, turned right away, and began to talk between themselves.

I realized fully that Ted Clifford-Turner's complicity in this plot was a very courageous act. It might indeed have caused a tiff between the two business partners and friends, so for the remainder of the luncheon I switched back to episodes that I had heard in my boyhood of Foster and his cricketing pals. Then we all three slunk out. Their Lordships did not even raise their heads to see us go. Charles, with that sixth sense of his which made him one of the most famous restaurateurs in London, must have realized that there was something electric in the atmosphere at our table, for he barely nodded his head as we went by.

Next year Foster invited me to his box at Lord's, which was next to that of C. B. Fry, so it was obvious that this charming English gentleman, who is now dead, bore me no ill will.

I pressed for a meeting with the Maharajah Jam Sahib of Navagwana, mentioning that his uncle had given me luncheon three weeks before his death. The Maharajah's entourage hesitated. They didn't like the press attention they were receiving, especially from the *Daily Mail*.

It was now 1947. I was living at Ponton, near Grantham. Somebody thought that Bedford might be a suitable place for a meeting between me and the Maharajah, somewhere we could both reach quite easily and without loss of face. And this was duly arranged. I drove myself to Bedford, accompanied only by my managing director, Mr. Odds. In courtesy we arrived early and were shown up to the hotel sitting room engaged for our secret meeting. We had a few bottles of Krug '29 put on ice. Suddenly there was a stir outside and a little deferential handclapping. We rushed to the window and saw descending from the first of two huge hired Daimlers a truly magnificent figure in the full regalia of his rank. To please lesser mortals, and to give children a treat, he even threw aside his superb black silk travelling cloak and exposed his glittering tunic to view. All could see that instead of buttons the tunic had luscious great cherries all down the front—or were they huge rubies?

An hour passed in reminiscence about how my uncles and Ranji – a forgotten name now – used to enjoy their carefree cricketing days together. The champagne began to work and the Maharajah said, "My uncle brought me up to believe that the British could be very bossy but thought they were the salt of the earth, particularly in Empire administration. They were, my uncle said, incorruptible. England's greatness was really based on her cadet class and on the great upper middle class that marched along beside it. Sixty or seventy preparatory schools tearing boys seven or eight years old away from their doting mothers and nannies and starting to teach them that inflexible but kindly discipline which was the first big stage in making them into men – and gentlemen. Above all, into English gentlemen. It was the proud heritage of English gentlemen to rule one-quarter of the entire globe. So the toughening-up process, the preliminary training, could not start too soon. Though not actually put into words, it was clearly understood by all – the great Ranji often said this, that there were really no gentlemen, no God-sent rulers born except those with a British passport. After one year at preparatory school the little blighters had forgotten all the soft comforts of home and became quite intolerant when mummies and nannies fussed over them during the holidays. The great scheme was beginning to work. The tempo of turning the screw was gradually increased and after five years thousands of potential rulers were pushed off into a score of great public schools, many of which specialized in training these hardened youths into the various branches of Empire ruling. Some for the Indian or Egyptian Civil Service, some for the Colonial Office, some for the Indian or other Empire armies, some for the legal departments, some for the public works departments, some for the East and West African Police, some for the Army and Navy of the motherland herself. One or two of the schools which educated the spawn of the rich and noble specialized in those forms of Empire ruling requiring large private (so-called) incomes—the Foreign Office, the classier regiments which surround the Monarch on glittering occasions, the 12th Indian Cavalry, and so on. No other nation in the world had ever begun to try doing the job so thoroughly. And the boys and their parents just took it as a matter of course. Probably never gave it a thought. 'Theirs not to reason why.' "

The Maharajah was silent. I knew that his uncle, Ranji, had loved all this. Ranji told me the last time I saw him a month or so before he died that at his first cricket match in England he was sure that people were watching to see whether he went into the Gentlemen's Dressing Room or the Players'. He had told Leonard Moon so at the time.

Yes, Ranji understood it all, and loved it. So his nephew, the Maharajah, and I got on fine for a first meeting. I was all the time thinking about the Maharajah's remark about the English being incorruptible. And in the end I got it out of him – in part. He was not getting a million pounds' worth of shares for his million pounds. Palms had to be greased, and greased heavily. Understandable, and usual, in all the lesser countries – but here in England! He just could not understand it. His uncle would turn in his grave.

I nearly fell off my chair in my effort to look cool and rather uninterested. Could I get him to mention even one name? But the Maharajah was getting cagey. I could see that he felt he had said too much already, and was regretting it. I changed the conversation back to general matters, then jumped suddenly back to the amount in question. He told me. £100,000. Were there several recipients? Answer "Yes." Were they men of importance – "Yes." It was enough – and my head was in a whirl.

More pleasantries and we parted.

After much thought on the way home, I telephoned that evening at his home, the only newspaper proprietor with whom I was then on Christian name terms, Lord Kemsley. I started to tell him just the gist but he interrupted me quickly.

"You fool, to start saying things like that over the phone," he said. "Let me think a moment. Yes, I have it. Tomorrow I'll send to see you up at Grantham one of my personal assistants. His name's Pawle. You can tell him the whole story and then he can report back to me."

The next day Gerald Pawle duly arrived, was told my story, reported back to Lord Kemsley. Within forty-eight hours came Gomer Kemsley's advice: "Don't touch it. You are fishing in deeper waters than you know. It could be highly dangerous for you. Try to forget all about it unless some clear and definite piece of evidence falls into your hands. If that were to happen, come and see me straight away."

But I was not only a fool. I was an obstinate fool. I sent word to Lord Kemsley that I had anticipated this advice and was sure it was excellent – but I wasn't going to take it. Bearing in mind the part they had played in very difficult waters over the Abdication of King Edward VIII, I chanced my arm and went to see Allen & Overy, the solicitors. They were completely unknown to me personally, and I to them, but the partner I saw quickly brought our interview to a close, saying that he wished to consult one of the senior partners. Within a day I was being cross-examined by both the senior partners, who had built up the firm. I had not mentioned Lord Kemsley, and entirely independently their advice was the same as his. Again, the fool did not take it.

Allen & Overy were however prepared to act for me and advise me. In particular, they instructed me in the rudiments of the laws on libel and slander. It was going to cost me a lot of money in legal fees, to get nowhere. They must bring in Mr. Valentine Holmes to talk to me severely, and I must say nothing, write nothing, without his prior permission. Valentine Holmes was the leading KC on libel and slander.

And we had no evidence. Worse was to follow. Lord Woolton, whom I had not then met, went to see the Maharajah. Then he came to see me. He told me that the Indian Prince did not deny my story but that he most firmly and decidedly refused to confirm it. There was too much of the British gentleman in the Maharajah for him to tell a lie. It was palpably obvious to Woolton that the Maharajah bitterly regretted ever having said anything to me and Mr. Odds and had taken top legal advice as to what to say to Woolton.

Anyone with the slightest common sense would have called it a day at this point, but I am not blessed with common sense, it seems.

Meanwhile – and even today I don't know how, because I was tightly muzzled by Allen & Overy – whispers were obviously going round in a very rarified circle of perhaps a dozen or so persons. Lord Beaverbrook rang me up and said that if even one tenth of what he had heard was correct, I was the biggest fool in Christendom. He wasn't scared of much, he said, but he'd be scared stiff if he was in my shoes. (These were his actual words according to notes I took at the time.) And that was the end of a very short, and one-sided, telephone conversation. "The Lord" didn't waste his time conversing with underlings, but he had no use for rank in any organization. If he wanted to talk to an underling, he did so. Not for him the usual channels of seniority.

The ripples of the pool were obviously widening and MPs less exalted than Oliver Lyttelton or Lord Winterton came to see me asking that I should tell them at first hand the gist of what this was all about.

I was also approached by several self-publicity seekers outside Parliament, each of whom would have liked to tell the Press that he was the first to know that there was really quite a story to be told and that he would tell it, but none of them got anything from me.

Allen & Overy had made it quite plain that if there had been any funny business the only way to prove it was to have a full scale Board of Trade enquiry, authorized by Parliament, when all the books, papers, memoranda, etc., would be seized and all individuals concerned cross-examined by top-grade professional people. This would be very, very far from easy, particularly if my wild assumptions had an atom of foundation in them. I somehow felt that between my first friendly meeting with Cripps and my second chilly one, Sir Stafford, that paragon of rectitude, had come across something that worried him, something concerning his own side. So he wanted Barford squashed, right out of sight, good and proper.

The next step in this one-man tussle, therefore, was to enlist the support of leading members of the Opposition in the House of Commons to press for a Board of Trade Enquiry.

I am wrong in calling it a one-man tussle. Some time before this, I had acquired a most doughty and courageous confidante, and ally, in the shape of Lord Brownlow, whose seat, Belton House, is near Grantham. Lord Brownlow and I were very old friends. Brownlow is a very able, clear-sighted man, with the courage of his convictions, so he was among the first to hear of my wild imaginings. By this time he was fully primed, and threw himself into the fight alongside me. He had the personal contacts which I, naturally, lacked. The easy entrée to where I could not get without great effort and preparation.

And whereas I was tightly muzzled, Lord Brownlow could talk freely. Which he did.

Allen & Overy reminded me that I had applied for the ex-government factories at Grantham on the usual "easy terms", presumably to make money for Aveling-Barford, of which I was dictator as well as largest shareholder. They pointed out that, on the other hand, Perry Brownlow was entirely disinterested, and that nothing could therefore be pinned on him. Plenty could be pinned on me, and might well be before I was much older, and Allen & Overy did not hesitate to keep on reminding me of that.

I talked to a few MPs in a most guarded and correct manner, through my muzzle, hoping that I was getting enough air through to excite their interest and curiosity. Oliver Lyttelton, the previous President of the Board of Trade, who had gone into the matter of these factories deeply and personally before confirming Dr. Hugh Dalton's allocation of them to me, was much interested. Lord Winterton also came in stoutly.

Eventually I was summoned before the 1922 Committee and really put through the hoop. The stage was now set. The Tories, it was agreed, would ask for a Board of Trade Enquiry into the matter of the Grantham factories, using a form of words suggested by me.

At this point a curious incident interposes itself. I still don't know whether there was any substance in it. But a senior member of the Press Gallery, a man who had looked down with disgust upon many successive bunches of legislators cringing under the lashes of their respective chief whips, an elderly and respected chap, told me that there was an unwritten law which had fallen into disuse simply because, as far as his memory went, there had been no occasion for any political party to use it. This unwritten law was that if the Leader of the Opposition himself, in person, asked for a Board of Trade Enquiry, then the Party in power would grant it, if only as a matter of courtesy, based upon age-old custom.

Mr. Anthony Eden was then Leader of the Opposition. I had just met him in my early twenties, but I felt that he wouldn't now remember my face or my name. Nobody among my tiny band of friendly MPS seemed to have heard of the old press guy's story, but all the same I implored them to try to get Mr. Eden to make the formal request personally.

He wouldn't. I am sure our case was not put adequately to him. Labour members were already saying "This chap Barford, who-ever he is, is just trying to waste the time of the Mother of Parliaments to line his own pockets. And by all accounts he's rich enough already. Let's get on with the real thing, good juicy busi-ness like giving away great slabs of the British Empire and alien-ating the rest of it."

If Anthony Eden had made the formal request as Leader of His Majesty's Opposition, instead of Oliver Lyttelton, the result might have been different. I just don't know.

As it was, it was Lyttelton who asked for a Board of Trade Enquiry, and the request was refused. Sir Stafford Cripps said some very acid and biting things about me, glancing from time to time to where I was sitting with Lord Woolton in the Distin-guished Strangers' Gallery. Another pal from the Press Gallery told me afterwards that I had one consolation: he had never in all these years there heard Cripps bother himself enough to make such an attack on an individual.

Everyone but me had known all along that failure was inevit-able. So far as I know no one person in parliamentary history has even attempted a similar action. My cousin, Gerald Upjohn – later Lord Justice Upjohn – had been engaged in a case of alleged political bribery, involving a mere suit of clothes. It was called, I think, the Lynsky case, and attracted tremendous publicity and interest.

We were not entirely defeated – not yet. Oliver Lyttelton and company put the Grantham factories case down for Question Time. They added a rider appealing to the President of the Board of Trade to "lay the papers on the table" so that members of all parties could see for themselves something of what had happened. This, they insisted, was only fair.

Of course, only about a dozen people had the slightest idea what it was all about. The whole thing was completely muzzled, cloaked, and obscured by the fear of libel and slander actions, or defamation of character.

Nothing more infuriating or exasperating could possibly have happened to me. The press had given up completely many months before. Naturally they didn't have the foggiest notion what was happening, if anything, and presumably the newspaper magnates kept to themselves anything they knew or suspected. My original formal application for the Grantham factories was in 1945, but the public controversy did not start until nearly two years later.

The publicity now had to be confined to the tame and uninteresting little story that this chap Barford wanted the Grantham factories, which were worth only about £400,000, for his personal gain. It was understandable that Barford was annoyed about the whole thing, but why drag Parliament into such a trivial matter? Cripps was President of the Board of Trade, and could allocate the factories to whomever he liked. Damn Barford. He's got a bee in his bonnet. That appeared to be the press view too, so they didn't even mention him. But the Maharajah and his million pounds, and his glittering tunic with rubies the size of cherries all down the front – he was real meat and drink for millions of readers. Mr. John Hall and his editor, on the *Daily Mail*, were right about that, though I don't think Mr. Hall ever caught sight of the cherries because the Maharajah and his suite embarked in their black Daimlers from the staff entrance of the hotel.

Nevertheless, Question Time in the House of Commons that day was a lively affair. Cripps, it seemed, had been anxious that Barford should be dried up at once and then Lyttelton and Winterton would have to stop needling him about that silly factory at Grantham. When the People's Car venture foundered Cripps felt he needed a new customer very quickly for the Grantham factories. A man named Sidney Cotton came forward and the factories were allocated to him straight away. Cripps made the necessary announcement himself, two days before the appointed day when questions were to be asked. A neat bit of work. The whole affair was over. Any questions now would be a damp squib. His chaps, for once, had worked with speed. He would never hear of Barford again.

The day before Lyttelton was to ask his questions the *Financial Times* carried a statement to the effect that the government factories at Grantham had been allocated to Mr. Sidney Cotton for the manufacture of agricultural tractors and other machinery. All very right and proper too. Agriculture is the backbone of the country. But someone on the staff of the *Financial Times* read that sentence and scratched his head. He was certain that a Sidney Cotton had gone broke in somewhat questionable circumstances. He phoned me, and then he told his boss what he suspected. He was given permission to search the files. In two hours he had found the entry he was looking for. The name was Sidney Cotton. But was it the right Sidney Cotton? He had to be sure. He went on searching, and I kept phoning him for a yes or no – a ten-second conversation every hour. No good news by the time I left for the House of Commons at 1.30 and by 2.30 some other questions had been answered and the silly business of the Grantham factories came up. Cripps got up ostentatiously and left the Chamber with a half-wave of his hand towards Belcher. Even I, who knew practically nothing of House of Commons procedure, realized that Sir Stafford was telling both sides of the House that he had had enough of this small-time matter and had deputed Belcher, Parliamentary Secretary to the Board of Trade, I think, to handle it.

Belcher got up and more or less paraphrased Cripps' previous strictures upon me, but in milder language. Honourable members must surely by now be bored with the whole affair but since so eminent an ex-President of the Board of Trade as Mr. Oliver Lyttelton kept pecking away at this question, then the Government's attitude must once again be repeated.

In the view of his department, Belcher said, this trivial affair started as no more than a private dispute between the heads of two businesses which between them employed most of the inhabitants of the small town of Grantham. Each wanted the government factory. Grantham Productions had now dropped out, so the permanent officials of the Board of Trade had advised Sir Stafford to allocate the Grantham factories to a most suitable applicant, Mr. Sidney Cotton. His department, Mr. Belcher went on, had been

Dear Mr Barford.

I am most grateful
for your letter of August
25th.

I entirely appreciate your
feeling of irritation, which I
should no doubt share when I
in your position.

It is because of what you
say in the last paragraph of
your letter that I was anxious
to bring finality into this
matter and I shall certainly
see that the findings are
given full publicity.

By thanks to you for
your understanding acquiescence.

Yours S. /

into all the relevant facts most thoroughly, both in regard to Mr. Cotton himself and his plans. The incident was, therefore, now closed and the House could turn to other business.

Cripps therefore returned – for the other business. Suddenly there was a stir. An official had almost run into the Chamber waving a slip of paper frantically in the direction of Oliver Lyttelton (now Lord Chandos). And a chap I knew slightly appeared in a gallery and was concentrating upon the progress of this slip of paper. It was Lord Moore of the *Financial Times* – now Lord Drogheda – so I knew something of value had been found out. The House paused while this slip of paper was passed along. Oliver glanced at it, rose, caught the Speaker's eye, and then addressed Sir Stafford Cripps.

"Is this Mr. Sidney Cotton," he said, "who has just been the subject of such fulsome praise, the same Sidney Cotton who was adjudged bankrupt three years ago and about whom some pretty nasty things were said at his public examination?"

Cripps looked aghast, struggled to his feet, looked at Belcher, then at Lyttelton, said, "I don't know," and sat down again. And now the fur really began to fly. The almost empty benches began to fill. Honourable members stopped snoring, and about six from all parts of the House tried to catch the Speaker's eye at once. The press leant forward and hoped that at last they would learn at least something of what all this was about and why Oliver Lyttelton was bothering himself about so apparently trivial an issue. But they were to be disappointed. Five minutes of hot air and it was all over. Finally, this time.

Four days later, Sidney Cotton telephoned me asking me to take luncheon with him. I was curious about the man, so I accepted, on the understanding that we shared the bill. So next day we met at the Mirabelle in Curzon Street. Cotton told me that three years previously he had had a piece of real bad luck. Some business associates had double-crossed him. He had, however, seen Belcher, and other high officials at the Board of Trade, and left documents proving his personal innocence. He was in the clear, and the allocation of the factories to him would stand. Furthermore, Sir Stafford Cripps had personally agreed at the start of Cotton's rushed negotiations with the Board of Trade, that Grantham Productions original huge allocation of steel would be passed on to Cotton – and this, in 1947, was an immensely valuable asset. Cripps and the Board of Trade dare not let him down now. After this failure the Board of Trade was as concerned as Cotton himself that Cotton's venture should be a resounding success. Everything that the Government could let him have, would be his. Labour would be transferred, houses built, and topmost priority accorded for allocations all round. The Ministry of Agriculture would help him sell his tractors. It would appear, in fact, that he planned to use officials of the Ministry of Agriculture as unpaid salesmen and demonstrators. The ball was at his feet. He had not misled the Board of Trade. If they had asked him whether he was the Sidney Cotton who had gone bankrupt three years before, he would have said yes. But they did not ask him. The mention of this subject in the course of question time debate was turning out very much to Cotton's advantage. The Board of Trade just dared not face the possibility of another failure like the £100 car. So, in all, Cotton was sitting very pretty indeed.

Only one thing worried him a little. He was not really a production man, not really an engineer. He was a financier. He was going to put a proposition before me. He suggested that he should continue everything as it was until he had got the factory all legally tied up in his name, with his steel allocations, his priorities, and so on. On this he would be glad of my expert advice. He had already decided to ask the Board of Trade for an unsecured loan of a million pounds for fifteen years, at a very low rate of interest, and the Board would not dare to refuse him. If I thought of anything else, maybe I could telephone him.

At this stage I mildly enquired why he was telling me all this and asking my advice. What was his proposition?

He had already told me, he replied, that he was a financier. The Board of Trade had already agreed to sell him the Grantham factories for £110,000 – not much over a half of the figure I had offered the Board of Trade under Dalton and Lyttelton, which meant that he, Cotton, felt he might well have made an unrealized profit of £90,000. And he paused to explain to me, an ordinary chap, what financiers meant by the term "unrealized profit".

Then he said he would come right out now with his suggestion, which would suit us both, and particularly me, absolutely splendidly. He then proceeded to put a business proposition to me, the details of which left me speechless.

I rose from the table, leaving my plate unfinished, bade Mr. Cotton good day, bowed to avoid shaking hands, and left the restaurant, telling the waiter, who knew me well, to post the bill to me. I went back to my flat, rang up Lord Kemsley, told him very briefly what had happened, and said that if he would feature it on the front page of the newspapers in his group, he could have the exclusive story. He did this, together with a photograph of myself.

As I have already explained, there had been nothing about my original, or subsequent, application for the Grantham factories which any editor, by any stretch of the imagination, could regard as newspaper material. Perhaps the Press Gallery in the House of Commons might at some stage have spent a minute or two reflecting that there might be a story behind Oliver Lyttelton's action in flogging for so long an apparently dead horse – but what? They had completely nix to go on, so they didn't waste any time on it. Nor would they now. Defeat was final and complete.

I had been working on this last stage of the battle for ten months. MPS would come and see me at my flat in the evenings. But what could I tell them through my muzzle, except to hint darkly and then have to refuse to answer their very natural and reasonable questions? Or I would go down to the House to keep an appointment with an MP. With each one of them it was a case of starting all over again from scratch, with nothing to tell but my silly little cover story. So they just thought I was trying to make money for myself, whereas actually I had given up any idea of the factories directly the Maharajah told me of that £100,000. Compared to that shock the factories and everything connected with them seemed trivial and tame to me. I was concerned only with unearthing the true story of where the Maharajah's £100,000 had gone to.

I had never worked so hard before, or since, on something that was additional to my regular job as boss of Aveling-Barford, so I feel it is essential to tell this story in my reminiscences.

But I hold no animosity to those who opposed me – I re-learned a valuable lesson, "Don't attempt the impossible."

The major result of all my expenditure of effort, plus a vast amount of money, was that I suffered a heart attack in the court-yard of the Savoy Hotel.

At the outset it looked bad, as the heart specialists gave me three to six months to put my earthly affairs in order, but after a few months I started to get better and a couple of years later I was completely recovered.

I am very, very lucky.

CHAPTER SIX

AVELING-BARFORD OPERATIONS

I HAVE already mentioned that forty per cent of the machine-gun carriers Lord Gort had with him at Dunkirk were manufactured by us. Throughout the war we were solely an armaments factory, turning out machine-gun carriers. What we should have been doing, at least at the latter part of the war, was manufacture in England the big American Euclid trucks which were being brought in convoy across the perilous Atlantic. But the brass hats didn't see it that way.

The result of it all was that we had to build up our peacetime trade practically from scratch in 1945. We also had to try to get back as quickly as possible all those chaps who had gone to war in 1939 and who had acquitted themselves so well in the great struggle.

During the war years considerable progress had been made in engineering techniques, and I wanted to get going as fast as possible so that we could take advantage of all the latest developments. All things considered our management did a splendid job and in 1947 we launched a completely new range of road rollers embracing the newest techniques and materials.

The war years had also seen immense strides forward in the design and use of machines for the civil engineering industry. Large dumpers were being supplied to the big public works contractors, for use in quarries, open-cast mining, and so on. Just before the war we had introduced a dumper with a capacity of $4\frac{1}{2}$ cubic yards. The users wanted now a machine at least twice that size, so we obliged. We also started making graders, our first range being manufactured under licence from a leading American manufacturer, the Austin Western Company of Aurora, Illinois.

We had made two issues of capital during the war, to replace the huge drains upon our legitimate profits caused by stupid and unfair taxation. As a result our paid-up Ordinary capital had increased from £200,000 in 1939 to £375,000 in 1945, all in 5s. shares.

Our new ventures sold well but because we had to start again virtually from scratch it was not until 1957 that we had really dug ourselves in both at home and abroad. For the first eight or nine years after the war my financial policy was to pay small dividends so as to retain as much capital as possible to develop and enlarge the business. I felt it necessary to alter this policy around 1954, so as to get our shares up to a level at which we could acquire other and smaller businesses in exchange for our own shares, and to provide a better basis upon which to raise money from the public.

In 1954, therefore, we made a Bonus Issue of two shares for one, thus increasing our paid-up capital to £1,125,000. In 1956 we issued £600,000 of Redeemable Debenture Stock, and in 1962 we made a Rights Issue which had the effect of bringing in further capital to the tune of another £1,125,000 and raising the paid-up capital to £2,250,000. Still all in 5s. shares nominal. Later we issued £2,000,000 of Convertible Debenture Stock and at the same time redeemed our £600,000 of Debentures. As a result of all this the capital employed rose from £2,600,000 in 1951 to £9,750,000 in 1965. These figures are on book values. A revaluation at today's figures would show a very substantial surplus. The figures also include both £2,000,000 of Debenture Stock and other advances amounting to well over £1,000,000. This is not strict accountancy but it gives a truer picture since all this money is actively employed in the business.

Although no country in the world is more dependent upon its exports than Britain, the attitude of successive governments has been words, words, words, rather than deeds. Every single year since the war I hammered away at this simple truth upon such occasions as my speeches to the shareholders at each Annual General Meeting. Here is a typical example, a speech I made in June 1948:

"The proposed final dividend of ten per cent, less tax, means that the total distribution for the year and a half is equivalent to slightly over fifteen per cent per annum. These dividends, paid to some 2,200 shareholders, represent about 4d. in the £ on turnover and slightly above three per cent on the real capital employed in the business.

To represent capital as a grasping and avaricious ogre is a mischievous misrepresentation. In the main, capital is provided by hundreds of thousands of citizens of moderate means, who play their part manfully, locally, and nationally in this England of ours. They invest some of their savings for their old age in concerns which they hope will give them a higher return than the safety of government stocks. Though the cost of living and wages have nearly doubled, capital alone works for pre-war wages; yet the risk has increased, and increased substantially. Today a business can be bankrupted by government edict because, for instance, it cannot export enough or is not classed as sufficiently important through the temporary whim of some government department; or its profits can be turned into losses because it is allocated insufficient materials or supplies. I have never heard any suggestion that the shareholders should be compensated in such cases.

The worst that can be said of a shareholder is that he takes all the risk and if he succeeds, he takes a "rake off" half of which is deducted by law for income-tax. For your company, the rate of dividend has been reduced until it is now a net fifty per cent lower than in 1939, which means after an allowance has been made for the higher cost of living, that your dividend cheque has about one quarter of its pre-war purchasing power.

Much criticism is levelled today at private enterprise. Every experienced manager agrees that private enterprise is not perfect and that broad government directives are in the national interest: but public ownership and control through myriads of large and small officials leads only to national ruin and misery. This is, unfortunately, not a perfect world and hence the two-legged animal – man – was given a superior brain to overcome problems and difficulties. Private enterprise is the best (or the least bad) system yet devised and our energies should be devoted to improving it, rather than putting unworkable theories in its place.

There are three parties in industry – capital, management, and workers – united they stand, divided they fall. Basically the interests of all three are indivisible, because if the business falls, they all fall. Left alone to comply with fair national agreements reached between employers and employed, these three parties in a decent and average business can get along very well and almost all

83

difficulties that arise are surmounted with good old-fashioned British humour.

Unless our rulers will realize that the national interest demands – I stress the word demands – that they shall encourage industry and management instead of hampering it, we shall be faced with the misery of mass unemployment and empty bellies. Hard words, but only those who have never made a success, even of a coffee stall, will disagree with me.

The Government spend their time blaming everybody but themselves for the lamentable state in which our great country finds itself.

I make no apology for speaking on national affairs, because here again industry and the country are indivisible. The State has no capital. Each year we must produce enough foreign currency to pay for our imports of food and essential raw materials. Industry, and particularly export industry must have every help and encouragement, and in my view it is going to need it during the next few years.

From now onwards the cost of production is of paramount importance. Even if sold at cost, many British goods are too expensive to find buyers in export markets. We are up against it ourselves. The management of your enterprise is naturally much concerned that the end of the sellers' market finds us losing large and important contracts abroad at prices below our costs.

What is the total cost of the largest standing army Britain has ever known in time of peace? I refer of course to the army of officialdom now numbering over two millions. To this vast overhead must be added the counter-overhead of the great increase in staff necessitated in your business and every other to deal with officialdom – again I do not attack the individuals but the system. All this cost is added to every machine we, or anybody else, exports. Broad directives are all that are necessary. Make the directors and the management responsible for loyal interpretation. If they fail, then pillory them publicly and give them the choice of describing themselves either as fools or knaves.

More able chairmen than I have given lucid examples of the frustration and real damage to export trade directly resulting from this mass bureaucracy. We therefore have the picture of poor old British industry, hampered and hindered from the rear at every step, staggering into a foreign land, pausing to gather strength to gamely wave its tattered flag before entering the arena against that phenomenon of modern world history – that young, virile enterprising free people – the United States of America. Well may we be thankful that the strongest ties of sentiment, blood, and tradition bind to England so many onlookers around that arena – a sentiment that a bad government here can shake but cannot break.

The choice is clear. Encourage and support management, capital, and free enterprise; then British industry, and your company I hope in particular, will have a sporting chance to catch up, equal, and pass its friendly rivals. Browbeat and hamstring British industry and its management, continue to stir up discord and strife, maintain the army of bureaucracy – the answer will be misery and empty bellies. Straight words, but do not think it cannot happen here. It can."

This speech received heavy and favourable press comment.

CHAPTER SEVEN

A BIG GOVERNMENT OFFER

A COUPLE of years after the war I was approached by what is now called the Ministry of Defence with a proposition for my consideration. It was that I should endeavour to gather a consortium of firms to manufacture a military tractor with allied equipment, such as bulldozers, so that, in the event of a Third World War, Britain would be independent of overseas supplies for army and air-force use.

Their proposition had obviously been the subject of several previous conferences and I wondered whether I was the first or last chap to be approached.

Their plan was that I should raise money in the City of London to lease a surplus government war-time factory, say in Coventry, then purchase government-owned surplus machine tools at attractive prices, receive a contribution towards development expenses, say fifty per cent, and be given a guaranteed order for 500 machines a year minimum for ten years. The balance of production could be sold by the new company at home or abroad in the normal way.

I didn't need to put my thinking cap on for that one, so I was able to reply that the only sort of terms I could discuss at a future meeting would be:

1) A ninety-nine-year lease of a suitable government factory on the usual war-time terms, currently being negotiated with others by my friend Sir Philip Warter, who was in charge of disposal of factories owned by the State. This was a fair rent based upon half the initial cost.

2) The State would own all the necessary machinery and equipment and we would lease them on terms similar to 1).

3) The State would also pay all the development costs, as it had done for war-time developments.

4) I wasn't interested in the 500 machines per annum suggestion, which might be cancelled or altered with a change of government.

It would be safer to have a firm order for 2,500 machines spread over five years with a cash down payment of half the estimated cost in advance to help with the costs of manufacture.

5) I agreed that the price paid should be cost plus twelve and a half per cent as certified by auditors.

It was obvious that my line of thinking was totally unacceptable to the meeting so I rose, shook hands all round and that was the end of that.

Two or three years later, I learned that a consortium of three concerns were working hard on a heavy duty tractor. They were Vickers, to build the chassis, Rolls-Royce to supply the engine, and Jack Olding & Co. Ltd. to advise on the design and handle the sales and service at home and overseas.

The powers-that-be and the Board of Trade in particular were delighted, so everybody who was likely to be interested in a heavy duty tractor knew what a treat was in store for them. But I suspected then, and I suspect still, that the Caterpillar Company in America were having a hell of a laugh about all this.

The Vickers Tractor duly emerged for general sale. It was highly praised by officialdom, and preliminary deliveries were made to the main export markets. But the answer was a lemon, if ever there was one.

After a period of the hard and gruelling work that the Caterpillar had always surmounted so well, the Vickers Tractors failed and failed again. Many were shipped back to England for rectification. The upshot of all this was that the tractor was taken out of production and the project abandoned, with great damage to British engineering prestige abroad and huge losses to the shareholders concerned.

I was lunching one day after this with Kit Hoare and Commander Sir Robert Micklem, the director of Vickers in charge of their northern engineering enterprises. Kit was the host and he asked Bob Micklem, without any beating about the bush, how much Vickers had lost over the tractor. Bob wisely refused to answer—and I was not surprised.

Aveling-Barford had then a tiny subsidiary company registered in Canada, consisting mainly of a house in Brule Gardens, Toronto, occupied by a grand chap, Patterson, the manager, his daughter as secretary, and perhaps two service engineers. It existed for the important purpose of appointing and supervising local distributors over the huge sparsely populated area.

One day I received an airmail letter from Patterson telling me as a matter of interest just the information that Kit Hoare had been anxious to know at that luncheon a few months previously. The then chairman of Vickers had called in for a drink at Brule Gardens and had told Patterson the Vickers side of the whole affair, including the losses sustained. And it was no light total, even for a huge group like Vickers to lose.

Now I must relate a story which makes Aveling-Barford very proud.

The late President Nasser gave vast publicity to the fact that the huge Aswan Dam Project was being built with Soviet money and machinery. However, it became necessary for Aveling-Barford machines to be rushed out – a fact duly noted by construction engineers throughout the world.

The BBC broadcast a programme on the project, during the course of which the commentator said: "The Aswan Dam is the biggest engineering feat in the world today. One of the heaviest jobs falls on the dumpers you are looking at now. They are not Russian machines. They are designed and built in England by Aveling-Barford. They work nearly twenty-four hours a day, with three shifts of drivers to each.

"They were delivered with Union Jacks painted on their huge bonnets, but these have been scraped off and Russian emblems substituted. They are among the leading heroes of this vast project which is being closely watched by civil engineering experts from all over the world."

The export trade has been the life-blood of Aveling-Barford and its predecessors for at least 100 years. When Britain ruled one quarter of the explored and inhabited areas of this planet, it was comparatively easy for her to become the workshop of the world. Until a few decades ago, the Director of Public Works had all public services and building in his control, even down to hospital equipment. If a planter or estate owner on one of the colonies wanted technical or mechanical advice, he went to the people best qualified and most willing to help with anything that benefited the colony – the Crown Agents, who, for their services, charged about two per cent.

People like my great-grandfather and grandfather, and many who built up larger enterprises, provided England with the workshop with which the Crown Agents could equip the colonies. Nowadays, the position is completely reversed. No longer is a quarter of the world willing to buy from us. We have to fight hard with Britain's competitors to sell anything.

From the moment I became chairman of Aveling-Barford in 1933, I concentrated almost exclusively on the export trade. About seventy-five per cent of our output went abroad – a percentage greatly in excess of the average. Our post-war products have been mainly earthmoving equipment, such as graders and dumpers—an industry that was developed in the USA where a huge opportunity naturally exists. After ten years of intense effort, Aveling-Barford succeeded in breaking the American monopoly in many export markets. This was a remarkable achievement when our size is compared with the American giants.

The American industry is dominated by some of the world's largest corporations, notably General Motors and the Caterpillar Tractor Company.

For some of my readers, I will explain that the great Caterpillar Company of the USA were the originators of the heavy track tractors, as opposed to the lighter wheeled tractors as used mainly for farming.

Caterpillar tractors are much more expensive, but they work in tough off-road conditions that would be impossible for the wheeled type. They are the largest and most important firm in the world in this specialized field, which includes bulldozers and allied construction equipment.

Their machines had been used extensively in the United States for many years, but the need for them and their variations, such as bulldozers, had not become apparent in England until about 1934/35. Then it was spearheaded by plans for airfield construction following the first glimmerings in Cabinet circles that this youngish chap Hitler might prove eventually to be somewhat of a menace.

So the agency for Caterpillar equipment was hawked up and down Berkeley Street in London, where many of the leading motor distributors and agents were, and are, still located.

I knew about this and thought I recognized some of the potential sales in England, but it happened two or three years too early for me. I was moving the infant Aveling-Barford Ltd. from Rochester to Grantham and my small sales staff were steam roller specialists and nothing else. We were manufacturers and sellers, at home and abroad, of British-built road rollers, and to become selling agents for American machinery might be very damaging at that stage of our development.

I had more than enough on my plate each and every day. My colleagues and my sales staff were adamant in their advice that I should not even consider applying for the distributorship, so I didn't – but with reluctance.

Jack Olding, a car agent in Audley Street, was appointed the sole distributor for England, and by using his brains he made a very considerable fortune out of it in a very few years alongside his pal Godfrey Davis, who had equally started from scratch in car hire and leasing.

Bernard Sunley was a third. The son of a head gardener, he also used his brains and energy, firstly in demolition and site clearance, in which he was not over-successful, or perhaps he expanded too fast for his financial backing – at any rate he was unable to pay for some Aveling-Barford dumpers which we had delivered to him in about 1937.

I mention this in no sense of criticism but so that my readers shall see that the really go-ahead chaps don't always strike gold at the first borehole. I liked and admired Bernard Sunley. You can't keep a good man down.

Bernard secured the distributorship for Euclid Dumpers which proved to be even more of a money-spinner than Caterpillar for Jack Olding. He acquired a small company named Blackwood Hodge and used this as a shell for the Euclid franchise, which covered not only Britain but most of what was formerly the British Empire.

Today, Blackwood Hodge is a large and very successful public company under expert management, and it goes from strength to strength. Euclid is an important division of General Motors, the world's largest corporation, and what they don't know about huge dumpers and other large earthmoving equipment is hardly worth knowing. And I, silly fool that I am, went into competition with them all over the world!

The Euclid Division of General Motors alone is probably about ten times as big as Aveling-Barford. But David is still fighting Goliath, and pretty successfully, too.

The executive heads of General Motors itself made it very plain to me in New York a year or so before I retired from active control of my "baby" Aveling-Barford that their Euclid Division had the same healthy, honourable competitive respect for me and my company as we have always held for them – the Big Boys.

The industry has now grown and there are competing manufacturers, mainly in European countries. But I cannot conceal my sense of pride that my "baby" is still gaining ground and meeting all competition face to face.

What is my advice to my younger and ambitious readers? Rightly or wrongly, I advise that there is a better living to be earned in distributorship, retailing, and honest service to machinery than in manufacture. The pros and cons are too obvious to warrant repetition here.

Towards the end of 1937, I became friendly with a chap of my own age who, by reason of his brain energy and drive, had become one of the active bosses of the Caterpillar organization. For the purpose of my anecdote, I will call him by the fictitious name of Frank.

For several months after Britain had declared war on Germany in September 1939 there was a phase which became known as the Phoney War. We later learned that the "Phoney" part was exclusive to us. Some brass hats and cabinet ministers were expecting overtures from Herr Hitler. Some of us underlings were expecting nothing of the sort.

It was during this period that Frank happened to be in London on business, so naturally we got together. World events had slowed demand, so even the great Caterpillar Company had spare manufacturing capacity at that particular time. As I have said elsewhere, I knew how desperately short we were of the fighting equipment that came within my sphere such as bren gun carriers and light tanks.

I took Frank to Grantham, where my factory was now exclusively devoted to the manufacture of bren gun carriers. Frank had a good look around with my works director, Mr. E. R. Howlett, and others, and that evening told me that, after a tooling-up period of say five or six months, Caterpillar could manufacture more than five times the Aveling-Barford output, plus a good quantity of tanks as well if the British wanted them.

The United States were, of course, neutral, and so free to supply both sides within their own government's limitations, which were a domestic matter for them. Frank went home a few days later, while I pressed for orders to be given to Caterpillar through our purchasing department in Washington. But I could not get anything definite in London other than that "the matter was in hand". Three or four months later, Frank was again on a flying visit to Europe.

He was disgusted. He had been offered a trial order of fifty bren gun carriers subject to this and subject to that. This was, to him, "just a nuisance of a tool room job. We are only interested in an order in thousands at a specified delivery per month. Our chaps all over Europe know that you are bloody well short of almost everything, and the Germans know it, too. We are neutral, but my mother is English and I am on your side. How can you help the British if they won't try to help themselves?"

My blood was up, good and proper. So I sought an interview with Beaverbrook for both of us.

Within five minutes, brass hats and others were summoned in the most peremptory manner, to be lashed by language that is unprintable. They were given orders and no opportunity to answer back. We were out of the little room at the end of the conference room at the Hotel Cecil within twenty minutes. Even Frank was aghast. As Beaverbrook was giving us his usual brusque handshake, Frank stammered: "You're Canadian aren't you, me Lord?"

He told me a few minutes later that he couldn't think of anything else to say!

CHAPTER EIGHT

EDDISON PLANT

In 1937 I had succeeded in making the three-year-old Aveling-Barford into a public company with a modest capital of £360,000. I was spending a number of solitary evenings each month in my sitting room at the George Hotel at Grantham deciding what I should cut out from this composite company and what new ideas I should consider.

Both I and my company were out of debt at last – a wonderful relief.

After my usual careful consideration by my moderate brain I decided that roller hire (to be followed by hiring similar plant) would be a profitable additional asset to my company and that is how, somewhat later, after a tough series of events between Ruston & Hornsby of Lincoln, Ruston-Bucyrus, also of Lincoln, and Bucyrus of USA, I felt myself personally obliged (since I was no longer penniless) to take over the Eddison Steam Roller Company which owned and hired about 400 steam rollers with a sleeping van each for the driver.

I was very reluctant to do this. I had negotiated the purchase purely as a spearhead for hiring Ruston-Bucyrus excavators and Aveling-Barford rollers, with future expansion in mind, by allowing leading manufacturers of another construction plant to join and put up additional capital. Ruston & Hornsby said they were interested to come in as a third partner with their railcars. There would then be plenty of capital, and Eddison's would be the kicking off point with its large fleet of steam rollers, though steam rollers were already becoming increasingly replaced by diesel rollers.

I had seen the writing on the wall and had already stopped the manufacture of steam rollers at Grantham.

My thinking convinced me that existing steam rollers, purchased at the right price, could earn a businesslike return on capital if they were used for between seven and ten years. By then they would have been written off annually in Eddison balance sheets and replaced by diesel rollers. In other words, the profits earned by 400 steam rollers would pay for annual purchases of diesel rollers – particularly second-hand machines.

I had gone a long way in the negotiations when (for reasons which I understood), Ruston-Bucyrus suddenly withdrew, followed by Ruston & Hornsby, and I was left alone as the sole instigator. Ruston & Hornsby were then the largest shareholder in Aveling-Barford, apart from myself. They felt that the whole thing should be dropped.

Ruston & Hornsby originally owned fifty-two per cent in Aveling-Barford and two of the four directors were their nominees.

I paid £12,000 for the worthless share capital of Eddisons and guaranteed (by a deposit of some Aveling-Barford shares) £50,000 of their overdraft and loans, which were well over £150,000 – or more than the saleable value of the business.

I thought I had lost my £12,000 and probably a slice of my guarantee, but events did not work out that way. I found some small saleable assets, such as cottages, cut the overheads and, in a couple of years, the losses turned to profits. Then the whole concern lay more or less fallow during the war, so far as I, the owner, was concerned, because I was otherwise occupied, mainly on the "dollar a year basis".

In 1947 I had my major heart attack. Recovering from it, I took June, my wife, her two children and my three to the Spithead Hotel at Bembridge, on the Isle of Wight, where I could not stagger even as far as the beach.

Meanwhile, I was hardly interested in a stern report from Price Waterhouse, the accountants. Eddison Plant (as I had renamed it) was being audited and the net profits looked like being £70–75,000 for that year, and though I had given certain shares to the management, I might well have £40,000 to £50,000 added to my income and surtax returns for that year, plus lesser sums for previous years. I knew that Eddisons were just getting on to their feet, but dying men must take serious note of top medical advice and clean up such sordid details as money before being

"Seated in State
On a Red Hot Plate
Between Pilate and Judas Iscariot".

So when I returned from Bembridge my then chauffeur helped me into a City office or two, and each time he appeared, one and a half hours later, and finding me in a conference room, brushing aside all opposition, he would gather up my papers and manhandle me back to my car.

As a result, I did not get much of a price for Eddisons. Fuller Horsey Sons & Cassel had valued the net assets at more than £450,000 on a very conservative basis, and they were among England's leading industrial valuers.

British Electric Traction offered me about seventy per cent of this valuation. I was feeling very ill and tired, for heart attacks really deserve the name of agony and you do not know even a minute in advance when they are coming. But, even so, I was not too far gone to remember from all the figures, which I knew by heart, that Eddison now had £55,000 in the bank—a change from the time when I had risked some of my hard-earned pelf to buy them up.

So, after two days largely resting in my flat, I telephoned my acceptance, but said that the shareholders were going to take out £50,000 in cash first, because I saw no reason for selling pounds sterling to BET at 15s. each.

I had never met Harley Drayton until all was signed and sealed, but this was obviously reported to him and he was amused and repeated it, because my friend Bobby Renwick telephoned me to arrange a threesome meeting. Harley treated me with considerable respect after that, told the story around the merchant banks in the City, and asked me to luncheon more times than I could fit in.

Why had nobody thought of doing this before? Several instances were recalled of selling shareholders who had, in effect, received less than par for their cash in the bank.

I have already said that I purchased all the Ordinary shares in this company for £12,000 cash. I considered there were good reasons for this, though the company's audited accounts showed clearly that it was insolvent and making small but increasing annual losses. Their bankers were very restive and threatening to put in a Receiver. Hence my guarantee of the £50,000.

I did not have to put in a penny, but it cleared the air miraculously with Eddisons' longstanding suppliers who, for a matter of years, had been reducing deliveries or telling Eddisons to "buy elsewhere" unless they could pay promptly for goods already supplied. Actually, we turned the losses into profits in two years (I had expected only to stop the losses in two years). So two years later I was able to withdraw my guarantee, leaving me with no "strings".

BET paid me £260,000 after I had just taken out £50,000 in cash. My personal "take" was less than this because, although I had put up all the money, I had given away a percentage of the shares, as I mentioned earlier. So it was not such a mouldy investment after all. The £12,000 had become £310,000 in a few years of active trading.

But if I had realized I was not going to die and not sold out in a hurry for not much more than half the real value during my six months "to put your affairs in order", I should certainly have got at least £700,000 and maybe much more. For our profits were going up rapidly each year, and at the same rate of progress were scheduled to pass very easily the £100,000 mark in two more years. By keeping the momentum at the same level, something well over a million would have been the lowest price I would have been offered say five years later.

So my small investment of twelve or thirteen years previously would by then have proved even less mouldy.

But I should not have sold because then I knew that I still had some life in me. And Harley Drayton said again and again in his speeches to his BET shareholders that their purchase of Eddison Plant was proving more profitable each year, so they were putting more capital into it. Harley had become a good friend and I enjoyed his company.

Really big capital gains are made at the early adventurous stage, such as Marks & Spencer, Charles Clore with Sears Holdings, Isaac Wolfson, Jack Cohen with his Tesco Stores, etc. And the same was true, too, two, three, or four generations ago with Harrods, Gamages, John Brown with shipbuilding, Wills with their tobacco, Players ditto, plus today's leading merchant bankers, whiz kids like Jim Slater "and all".

It is the early bird that catches the worm, and the earlier the better. The list is endless and new names crop up annually though my favourites are Moses on his Mount telling the people (iron lungs with no loud-speakers) just where they got off, and Elizabeth I of England, the Virgin Queen.

But one should never look backwards. Past experience has one value only – to profit by it next time.

CHAPTER NINE

ALAN GOOD

ALAN GOOD was a brilliant, youngish lawyer and accountant, who had made a considerable name for himself in the City of London during all the tangles and losses of the 1931/33 slump, and by about 1936 had achieved a status which gave him first-class city financial backing.

He was one of the many predecessors of those successful chaps who, in 1972, are known to have been more or less penniless about ten years earlier. History repeats itself time and time again in every sphere of achievement. Napoleon picked his young men well, and promoted them very quickly.

At what age did Marshal Ney die?

And what about Horatio on his bridge – how old was he?

And how old was my great hero Moses when he stood on his Mount and bellowed to tell all who were not too deaf to hear him just what to do and what not to do?

In other words, he told them (and got a hoarse throat in the process) just where they were to get on and where they were to get off. Posterity called this advice The Ten Commandments.

Alan Good had the same ideas as me – get some water or paper shares and then use his brainbox and common sense to turn the worthless share certificates into something of value. But he did it in a different way, and doubtless a more profitable one; he was not a lone wolf like me.

He had given enormous thought over a period so as to use most profitably his new-found City backing, and he saw among the office mail what looked like an opportunity – a smallish engineering firm whose main proprietor had recently died. He did the obvious snap investigation, for he knew even less about any form of engineering than Edward Barford, and made an equally snap offer on behalf of his backers and himself.

He learned of a prospect, he sniffed at it and if it seemed

probable that more drive and initiative would almost certainly result in more profitability, with real gains to work-people, staff, management, and shareholders, he dived in on terms which he was fairly confident would subsequently give a reasonable return for his own work and initiative, plus a subsequently realizable profit for his risk-taking backers in the City. In other words, his thinking and actions were a good thirty years before his time. He was pioneering personally in the mid thirties in a limited sphere what in the last few years has come to be known as the takeover bid.

I can personally vouch that he never told me that he had held long-winded official meetings or had access to audited figures or balance sheets, or opportunity for up to date valuations of fixed assets. For those were the days when practically nobody had even an approximate idea of what a particular business (often owned by the descendants of Grandfather X, less than fifty in number), was worth.

First, find your possible fish! A few discreet enquiries as to who collectively owned over fifty per cent of the business. A routine search charge (5s. at that time by Somerset House) as to the probate value per share agreed with the Inland Revenue following the latest death of a member of the owning family, and a lowest common denominator or guideline was known to Alan Good.

Then it was Alan's guess as to what he had to pay (money by backers) to gain control. It was his firm objective (I believe that) that everything should be open, above board, and amicable. Extra support for management, chairbound directors happily compensated mainly out of increased profits, etc.

His technique was obviously the product of his own astute brain, and it was easy for me to see, when I first met him about 1936 or early 1937, that he had developed the assurance and confidence of a leader of men. He had also graduated to a regular prominent table at luncheon in the Savoy Grill, where I first met him. I remember well that I found it an interesting first meeting also because I had done a bit of graduating myself in the same restaurant four or five years previously.

The Savoy Restaurant was very well known to be a luncheon haunt of many of the top brass in industry, and, generally speaking, the waiting staff, from the maître d'hôtel downwards, knew everybody and almost everybody knew each other, at any rate by sight.

The routine at the Savoy Restaurant at luncheon was the same as at the Savoy Grill after theatre in the evening – a half smile or a flick of the hand to one's equals, some form of obeisance to those much above you, but chaps only stood up if a female or a very high-up chap came to a complete halt for half a minute or so on his way to his own reserved table. It was all quite funny and correct, but a very amateur performance compared to the units of the Household Cavalry and the Brigade of Guards when they are equally on parade.

By about 1938, Alan Good and his backers owned several smallish but good engineering works, and found that they were mainly engaged in the same sort of activity, and maybe had been for several generations. I am purposely not giving any names or being more specific because sometimes he had only bought one big parcel of shares with the idea of buying control later at an equally attractive price.

This is where Edward Barford came in, and Alan Good wrote that he would like to meet me for a business luncheon at the Savoy.

After telling me over several evenings and weeks just what he wanted me to know and no more (a good deal of it had been known to me for two or three years previously), he said he was prepared to pay over the odds for a leading name to be king pin of his group of engineering companies. I had guessed a couple of conversations before that he didn't want my bright eyes. He wanted the "Aveling" name and goodwill, particularly in the British Empire.

He already had my published accounts for five years. Since these jottings are for the benefit (I hope) of the starter, I will explain that in offering shares through the Stock Exchange in 1937 one revealed Price Waterhouse's audited figures for just three years previously. In the current year, our monthly figures indicated profits at £140,000 p.a., and continuing to grow at about twenty per cent p.a.

In early 1939, I owned about fifty-five per cent, including those shares I had already given to my close relatives. I had bought seven per cent to add to the original forty-eight per cent that I had allocated to myself in 1933 as part of my deal with Ruston & Hornsby.

The upshot of these advances by Alan Good was as simple as pie. Through a leading firm of merchant bankers, endorsed by one of the leading joint stock banks, he and his backers offered me £650,000 cash for my fifty-five per cent. Very simple wording. No lawyers necessary at that stage. I just had to collect back, or make suitable arrangements, about any shares I had given away, so that Alan Good and partners became owners of fifty-five per cent of the Ordinary share capital of Aveling-Barford Ltd. at the date of their offer, which was to expire on some date in February 1939.

The only condition made by Alan Good's side was fifty per cent down against share certificates, etc., and the balance spread over eighteen months if they wished – but this was guaranteed both by the joint stock bank, equally with the leading merchant bank, together with appropriate interest.

Only then did I bring in lawyers, who said this is ninety-nine per cent as safe as the Bank of England. I well remember that they made a pun on the name "Good".

It is very much in my mind now – 1972 – some thirty-three years later that I was such a fool then as not to realize that this was a wonderful and amazing offer, which anyone but a dolt like me would have tied up legally and irrevocably within forty-eight hours.

It was all so simple for me. As the earlier parts of these jottings show, I have never been any sort of an engineer. I have never been a helpful chap about my own house – I think I could just replace a fuse wire, but I have never known how to locate exactly which one to replace. I have never replaced a washer on a tap or boiled an egg.

It was crystal clear that the sooner I got away from anything and everything that I was and am completely useless at, the better. If I accepted the offer of Alan Good and his backers I would be a rich man for the rest of my life – and much richer, I guessed, than most of my friends and acquaintances.

I have not checked it up, but in February 1939 more and more people were becoming increasingly of the opinion that another world war was very much on the cards, so Stock Exchange prices were nose-diving alarmingly. I could have stuck a pin blindfolded in a list of forty to sixty of sound leading investments here, in USA and Canada, with half, and kept the other for second thoughts when I got round to them.

I have always liked solid things like land and buildings, and have invested in them quite substantially since. At the Alan Good negotiation period almost all my eggs plus some overdraft were in one basket – Aveling-Barford Ltd.

At a very rough guess, and without being any more of a dolt than I am, I suppose the £650,000 in January or February 1939 would be around £6,500,000 in 1972. There was no need to speculate. All I had to do was to instruct a good firm of stockbrokers to give me a good wide spread of sixty-five leading companies and to invest £10,000 in each. Some will have gone up much more than ten times, others merely kept pace with inflation. But it is difficult for anyone to deny that £6,500,000 is a reasonable estimate. Even today, I should have been somewhat removed from the breadline.

But I am sure I could not have adventured out on my own in 1933 if I had not toughened myself and been toughened by my experiences, problems, and difficulties since I ran away from Rugby School in 1915.

So much for the sordid side – because money has never and will never interest me much. As I have said elsewhere in these jottings, my advice, for what it is worth, to younger chaps and their girls is to make enough straightforwardly and honestly in applying yourself to something you enjoy doing (which will make your girl happy, too).

And so I come back to what in my mind is the only real reason for any old washout to dictate his personal experiences in life. Tell what actually happened – my trials, tribulations, and errors, and how I have tried to learn not to make the same stupid mistakes more than twice.

My life – beginning, middle, and ending – has been very ordinary and my achievements almost nix. In this meandering of thoughts, ideas, and unfulfilled semi-ambitions I make no apology for repetition or anything else. Because my potential reader is also an ordinary chap – there are just millions of us in Britain alone and many more in the Americas and everywhere else where ordinary individuals of both sexes work decently and conscientiously to improve their own lot and thus the country of their birth or adoption. Any man or woman who is fortunate enough to hold citizenship in what we now term "a free country" should indeed count their blessings.

CHAPTER TEN

POLITICAL VIEWS

THE Labour movement – not the Labour Party, which is no longer the same thing – maintains an entirely outmoded image, an image which stems from the bad old days when workers wore cloth caps and hob-nailed boots. Labour – the movement, the ideal – looks backward, not forward. The lot of the weekly wage-earner has improved vastly during the last forty years or so, and at an ever-increasing rate. Quite right too. And the lot of the inherited rich has spiralled down at a proportionate rate. That's all right, so long as we don't let the pendulum swing too far, as it may have done over the last few years.

"We are all equal in the sight of the Lord" is one of my favourite phrases. But we are not equal, of course. The good Lord puts a good brain, a tough physique, the spark of ambition in a minority. I call it a talent. A boy can recognize it within him at an early age. Then it is up to the boy himself whether he develops his talent by working harder than his mates, and by rigid self-discipline. By not taking all the time off he can from school, and afterwards from work. By getting to the top in school-work, or in games. The competitive spirit.

The boy – or girl – with that is a national asset.

But the Labour ideal glosses over these solid facts of nature, pulling everything down to a level rather than giving a fair deal to the brighter, hard-working chap. They bullyrag the present for the faults of the past, these Labour idealists. They cannot or will not see the great march of progress.

In the dreary and overworked lives they then led, the cloth-cap army were the main supporters of such cruel practices as bear-baiting, cock-fighting, and coursing, with no means of escape for the hare. Further back still, they enjoyed seeing witches burned at the stake, men broken on the wheel, and grisly heads stuck on spikes at Tyburn Hill.

The Invicta Horse, the registered emblem of
Aveling-Barford Ltd. This sculpture, by Gilbert
Bayes, stands in the boardroom at Grantham.

The author—many, many years ago.

King George V talking to the author's
father, James Golby Barford, at the Royal Show in 1921.

Sir Alec Douglas-Home, then Prime Minister, paid a special visit to the Aveling-Barford works at Grantham in November 1963 (see page 145). He is seen here with the author.

Looking back from today, who can blame them? Their lives were one long misery of overwork. Conditions are very different now and today's manual worker would be among the first to be revolted at the cruelties of long ago. Changed for the better though things are, however, it seems to me a great pity that so very many honest, respected citizens, who are fine family men and women, allow themselves to be influenced by a tiny minority of dishonest loud-mouthed tub-thumpers. Most of these are in the pay of Communist governments, who find it easier and cheaper – and more successful – to disrupt a country economically from within than by waging war in the old-fashioned way.

Surely it is the work, effort, and enterprise of the intelligent chap that produces practically all the wealth with which to pay wages. Why then should it be the cornerstone of Labour thinking to tax the intelligent chap out of existence? I know, for instance, of a leading surgeon who works only six months each year because taxation would take almost all the rest if he worked a full eleven. He is a leader in his field, and his five months' holiday is a national loss, no less. These intelligent chaps have enabled wages to increase in step with the cost of living and prevent inflation.

Anyway, and this is the real point, today's working man is no longer a member of a huge cloth-cap army. He reads about other people's lives and problems with interest. He owns a television set, he goes abroad for his holidays, he runs a car. In fact, what has happened in this country since 1939 is probably the most remarkable case in world history of a peaceful revolution. Because it has been entirely bloodless and gradual, we don't seem to realize that it has come about nonetheless, or the extent of its significance. Yet in the past twenty-five years Britain has probably achieved far more than the French did in their bloodthirsty revolution. Wealth and spending power have been redistributed much more equitably. The people are healthier, their children are better educated, and the population as a whole lives under better circumstances, with more food, more leisure, and far more money, than ever before. As a result people are better equipped, physically and mentally, to play their part in the government of their locality or even their country. The struggle and wish of every man to better himself, to reach a higher social level, to give his children a better start in life than he had himself, all this underlines the fact that people are thinking more for themselves than ever before.

But while Labour, as a movement, looks backward, the Labour Party most certainly does not. At one time of course the two were indivisible, with organized Labour calling the tune and the Party its slave; but a radical change has now taken place. Whatever faults the Labour Government may have been guilty of, and whatever mistakes it made, one thing has been proved – namely, that Labour did form a government comprised of men of ability, and courage. Mr. Harold Wilson's men may lack experience, but they do not lack brains, as the scholarships to school and university they won as young men show. And this may have a big effect on the voting at the next General Election. At the last election, many solid and responsible citizens, I am sure, in the middle to lower income groups and dissatisfied with the Tory Government's lack of initiative and drive on the home front, but unable to see Labour as a responsible, patriotic alternative government, played safe and voted Tory. Will they do so again?

When Labour won the General Election of 1964, the crusted old Tories said that the end of the world had come. They ignored and brushed aside the fact that the Labour Party team included men of considerable learning and distinction. Those old diehards just did not want to know. In the words of the Gilbert and Sullivan song, they were born little Conservatives and that was good enough for all their lives. They have used their brains so little throughout their sheltered lives that they no longer have the capacity or intellect to think for themselves.

Britain needs today a leader who is not a politician, and I use the word politician very deliberately. Britain needs a common sense chap to lead his England and our England to "Set the People Free" and "Trust the People".

President Roosevelt aimed at his four freedoms, but he set his sights too high. They were: freedom of speech, freedom to worship, freedom from want, freedom from fear.

World history has taught us that dire national need produces a leader – just one man from the masses – previously unknown to his fellows.

I sometimes wonder whether we have just one Socialist Party in Britain, or two. Look at the Tory budgets, for instance, and

compare them with the Labour Party's budgets of twenty years ago.
Look at the main provisos of Sir Stafford Cripps' post-war budgets
and compare them with those of Mr. Reginald Maudling and his
successors when in office. Which budgets are the more socialist?

I defer to nobody in my conviction that the treatment of the
weekly wage-earner sixty years ago was a foul blot upon a great
Christian country. But is that any good reason for a swing of the
pendulum so far the other way that the Tories also now put heavy
penalties on brains, hard work, and initiative, whilst molly-
coddling the rest of the nation from the cradle to the grave? The
work-shy come in for an extra dose of this nauseating syrup.

Yes, the Tories have certainly done their full share of molly-
coddling the work-shy, the lazy, the unambitious, the real wrong-
uns, the people with so little feeling for their fellow-mortals that
they take every opportunity to lie in bed year after year, while
others do all the work for them—including exporting to bring in
foreign currency and buy food, so that those chaps need not go
hungry as they lie in bed.

The Labour Party is, of course, financed by the political levy
paid by every member of a trade union, unless he contracts out of
paying it. The finances of the Conservative Party, on the other
hand, are helped by substantial donations from business concerns.
Instead of an agreed levy, however, there is no yardstick at all for
the size of these donations. One firm may give £1,000, another
£500, and a third £50; and whatever they give, it may be quite out
of proportion to their earnings.

For a long time I have felt that some scale of giving should be
laid down. As a yardstick, or at least as a basis for discussion, it
occurred to me that a sum equal to what firms pay annually in fire
insurance would be reasonable. After all, the danger of disruption
to private enterprise through the actions of irresponsible Socialist
elements is much greater than the risk of fire. Nobody contracts
out of fire insurance, but very few factories are ever burned
down.

I mentioned my scheme many years ago to the late Lord Camrose. He suggested I write a letter, outlining my plans, to the
Daily Telegraph, which was then his personal property. He would
see to it that my letter was accompanied by a leading article on the
subject.

I wrote this letter, and publication was agreed. Then I went to Grantham, where I spent a lot of time those days.

At my hotel I was surprised to receive a message that Lord Woolton, whom I had not at that time met, wished to speak to me urgently on an important matter. I had to take the telephone call in a corner of the public lounge, not the best place for a serious discussion.

"As a matter of courtesy," said Lord Woolton, "Lord Camrose has told me of your suggestion, and of the letter he intends to print. I think this would be a very great mistake indeed. Lord Camrose refuses, however, to take your letter out, unless you give him or me your permission to do so. The newspaper is on the point of going to press, but there is still time to remove the letter and replace it with something else, if you agree."

"If that's your view," I told him, "then you have my permission to take out the letter."

Lord Woolton thanked me, and said he would like to see me when I got back to London.

I was incensed at this action, and I imagine that the editorial staff at the *Daily Telegraph* were even more incensed. On the following Saturday, however, I went to Abbey House, then the headquarters of the Conservative Party, to see Lord Woolton. He said that he much regretted upsetting my plan, but that he was sure his advice to me was sound. He was very glad that I had accepted it. He did not, however, say anything to make me change my view that my scheme was a good one, and that it, or something similar was needed. I feel the same today, some twenty-five years later. Firms should of course make their contributions openly and tell their shareholders, and the general public, what they have done. I often wonder what might have happened if my scheme for political fire insurance, as I called it, had been adopted.

A lot of people in Britain are dyed-in-the-wool Conservatives; and there is another great group who will always vote Labour. In between is a mass of people who are capable of being swayed. I don't think that private enterprise is ideal, but it has proved incomparably better than public ownership. And because of the rising standards of living with which private enterprise is associated, those undecided voters are probably predisposed to the Conservative side, or at any rate towards an experienced National Government.

If only there was a party that stood, not for Tory or Labour, or Liberal interests, but simply for Britain!

The present method of government by political parties, each representing a particular class or outlook, is surely approaching the end of its useful life in Britain. All that the average person really wants is freedom to choose professionals, men of experience, to govern the country for him. No one wants to take a direct part in the larger issues of the day without expert knowledge. But under the present system cabinet ministers know little or nothing about the vast organizations of which they are temporarily in charge. Their departments are run by professional civil servants, not by politicians. The politician, the minister, is merely a bird of passage, and regards himself as such. For the cabinet is like a game of musical chairs. Each minister is just a politician hoping to be promoted to another and more important Department of State. It doesn't matter which department, so long as it means promotion, and progress towards the greatest plum of all – the Premiership. The lesser departments, such as Transport, Housing, and Health, are stepping stones to the Inner Cabinet.

So the cabinet minister is no more than the titular head of his department, and the professional civil servants under him, who have spent the whole of their working lives in the department, accord him only the courtesy due to a minister of the Crown, plus some lip service. In its daily running the department goes on its own way, and apart from the permanent secretaries and their three to five top chaps, those who work in it remain entirely dis-interested in whoever happens to be the titular head. If written questions about his department are put down in the House of Commons, the permanent secretary and his aides write down the answers for him. The minister is just the mouthpiece.

But though the politicians have no qualifications to improve the efficiency of their departments, they have terrifying power as cabinet ministers and can take vitally important decisions, big enough very often to attract much public attention.

Take any fiasco. Who decides to recommend the Prime Minister and his Cabinet to scrap the whole plan? A professional politician. Or maybe a brace of them, if the thing is big enough to straddle two departments.

Surely it should then be the duty of the ministers involved to suspend temporarily all those very senior, and anonymous, service officials, and others, who so strongly recommend embarking on the project in the first place, and the heads who prepared the estimates; and then to probe the whole matter thoroughly, which should be very simple as only the heads of departments are concerned. After all, it is the heads who take all the praise, the titles, and the honours, when things go right. But when things go wrong, the "machine" shields them, and defends their very anonymity.

Anonymous professional top brass make recommendations involving huge sums of money, to be spent over a number of years, to politicians who happen at that moment to be the cabinet ministers concerned, men whose professional and technical knowledge is probably nil, but who have the power to recommend their cabinet colleagues and others equally ignorant to embark on this vast expenditure. Then another government comes to power and another ignoramus on the subject says to scrap the lot – especially if there is political capital to be made out of saying that it was all the fault of the previous government. A terrifying spectacle.

Where does the answer lie to all this? In some form of limited dictatorship?

Dictatorship is rightly an ugly word, but during the war Britain accepted it in all but name. At that time I dubbed Winston Churchill and Lord Beaverbrook Dictators Nos. One and Two and was not surprised that neither of them objected, for that is what they were. The Americans, equally rightly and equally loyally, accepted Roosevelt as a virtual dictator, although only a few years earlier he had been extremely unpopular amongst great masses of Americans. Both democracies, in fact, accepted a limited form of dictatorship because the urgency of war made it imperative that full freedom of action and absolute power should rest in the hands of a few men.

Are the problems and dangers of peace today all the less important? I think not.

My proposal is this: we should retain the present electoral system right up to cabinet level, or near it. Then the Party in power must choose an uneven number of men – say seven or nine – to become the limited dictators of the country. Once selected to office, these men would be there for seven years. Afterwards they would retire completely from public life, with a status and a pension, or other emoluments, roughly similar to those enjoyed by an ex-president of France. In this way, whilst ruling the country our limited dictators would be entirely free from all thought of future elections, or their own personal and political future. They would thus have nothing to bias them or persuade them to do anything other than what they felt would be best for the country, and full opportunity to set in motion reforms with benefits not at once obvious to the public. Dr. Beeching, for example, was widely criticized for all he tried to do for our railways. But now the verdict is very different. He attracted criticism for trying to put right the wrong caused by years and years of inertia and neglect.

And the blame must be laid at the doors of governments who often, and rather inevitably, look only as far as the next general election.

I played a tiny part in breaking through the red tape during the war, but in 1945 chaps like me left for our lawful peacetime activities and the Machine – the Establishment – regained its power and particularly its power over its Ministers.

In talks with Lord Woolton during 1946/1948 I tried to hammer my views home. Dear old Daddy Woolton used to laugh at my vehemence. His aides at the Tory Central Office looked down their noses at me and obviously hoped that the boss (Woolton) would tell me to dry up and that I was wasting their valuable time, but Woolton was rather fond of me – we had just been through quite a piece together over Grantham Productions Ltd., and what had happened to the Maharajah's missing £100,000.

In November 1964, I wrote to Mr. Joseph Godber, Conservative MP for Grantham and former Minister of Labour, outlining a plan by which the Conservatives could be returned at the next election with a sixty-to-eighty majority. The kernel of the plan was to project a policy of graduated tax reductions by a public relations campaign.

Mr. Godber passed on my letter to Lord Blakenham, then chairman of the Conservative Party, but the latter replied, "I must admit I am rather sceptical about the feasibility of presenting the electorate with a detailed programme of tax reductions in exactly the form he suggests. . . . On the other hand, I certainly am convinced that one of the things we must do in Opposition is to look at the machinery of government, and see if we cannot suggest more efficient and businesslike ways of running the administration. . . ."

I was so convinced that a policy of reduced taxation was the surest way of getting the Conservatives back into power, that I would not be put off by Lord Blakenham's rejection of my scheme, and on 11th December 1964, I wrote again to Mr. Godber.

One of the pressing indications for the need for a new policy, as I saw it, was the fact that the policies of the two major parties were almost identical.

"The last Election," I told Mr. Godber, "was just like Cassius Clay and Sonny Liston. Both contestants were sitting in the same corner. . . . Both parties were offering the electorate the same old tripe."

I went on to say that though I respected Lord Blakenham, I disagreed flatly with almost everything he said. I went on, "He winds up by saying that the electorate would respond directly to sound practical suggestions, etc. That is precisely what I am attempting to make."

I sent copies of this letter to Sir Alec Douglas-Home and Reggie Maudling, and a number of my friends, and in due course I had a reply from Sir Alec. He agreed with me that our country "can only be great by the individual initiative. . . . I am certain that after a period of government by the Socialists, the country will come to realize that central direction and central control get us nowhere."

But I was unrepentent and wrote telling Sir Alec so.

"The Labour Party cannot deny," I wrote, "that their policies necessarily entail more regimentation, more bureaucratic control, and less freedom for every citizen. The policy of the Tory Party should be precisely the opposite on all these counts, and this diametrically opposed policy should be rammed home and made crystal clear to every inhabitant of this country above the age of fourteen."

Sir Alec thanked me for my letter, but the Party did not take up my ideas; and when the Labour Government went to the country again, they were returned with an increased majority.

It seems to me that since that time some of my thoughts and suggestions of seven years ago have borne fruit—perhaps an old file fell out of a cupboard and someone read the papers to fill in the odd half hour! So that the reader may judge this for himself, here are my views which were written and circulated in 1964.

"Set The People Free"
"Trust The People"

I urge the Tory Party to promise to make a simple but fundamental change in the relationship between government plus its bureaucracy on the one hand and the citizen – all the people – on the other.

And when this fundamental change becomes fully operative (it could not be achieved in a twelve month) – the savings would be counted in the hundreds of million pounds per annum to be passed on to the citizen in sharply reduced taxation, both direct and indirect.

We need a managed economy – but not so much as we now have – but we are "managing" it in precisely the wrong way and every year the situation gets worse.

The Tory Party should adopt new basic principles and all legislation and the implementation of it by bureaucracy should be directed towards two very simple objectives which I state in a few words –

"Set the People Free"
"Trust the People"

Both with safeguards and spot checks at one tenth the cost of the present bureaucratic control the failures and abuses of which increase sharply as it becomes more detailed.

Set the People free.

"England is the land of the free" was a favoured theme in old time songs. Yet how free is the average citizen of Britain today, in his ordinary daily life? I reckon that without actually employing the methods of the "Gestapo", Britain's vast army of officialdom has been gradually tying up the ordinary citizen until he has become a pathetic cowed object who has forgotten what real freedom means. To ensure a managed economy, we do not need all this detail and form filling. We pay this army of officials and they are our servants, but a vast number of individuals in that army, particularly those in the middle ranks, have steadily and progressively persuaded themselves that they are small-time dictators. They bully the people they are supposed to serve and help.

Equally important is the existing power of the Civil Service to make laws without reference to Parliament. I am glad to see that this wrong situation, which has gradually been building itself up over a number of decades, is now attracting public attention. Bureaucrats both make important regulations and enforce them on the citizen. This is a frightening situation in a country which still prates of freedom.

It is absurd to suggest that the existing control of the nation by bureaucracy is in the best interests of the nation. Everyone has seen in their own daily lives examples of the inequalities, absurdities, and downright dishonesty that results. One need only instance the recent example of two elderly widowed sisters who had been forcibly deprived of their home and garden a number of years ago for some road or other improvement. The official plan changed and bureaucracy then resold the property for fifteen times as much as the compensation previously given. But the original owners don't get a penny. This is plain theft from a citizen by the Government through bureaucracy.

Trust the People.

Excess bureaucracy increases dishonesty and evasion thus defeating the objectives of legislation passed by Parliament. Why should not the Government take as its axiom that the citizen is honest – until proved otherwise.

Taxation is a very good example. The present system is a nightmare to the ordinary citizen and no doubt equally to the battalions of inspectors of taxes and their officials who are in the main only obeying their book of rules and regulations. The cost to the nation of this section of officialdom is enormous. Yet again the wrongdoer probably gets through the net whereas the average chap curses as he grapples on with all the form filling and detail.

On the new axiom that the average citizen is entitled to be considered honest, let him have the simplest possible form amalgamating everything including surtax. I guess that about ninety per cent of the detail work now necessary could be eliminated in this way. A small proportion of the present inspectors of taxes could be formed into flying squads. In many cases it will be clear to these experienced chaps from the simplified declarations they receive if anyone is trying to pull a fast one. So the flying squad should have powers to pounce on any individual where he suspects something fishy and in any event to make random spot checks on say, one in 200 taxpayers. If a chap is proved deliberately dishonest in his tax returns, then treat him with much greater severity than is at present used. Imprisonment always and such heavy fines as to deprive him of much more than his ill-gotten gains. The severity of these sentences plus the unwelcome publicity will be the greatest possible deterrent to others.

Adoption of principles similar to the above might well save three-quarters of the cost of tax collection.

The system of short general directives was much used during the war, particularly at the top by, for example, Churchill and Beaverbrook. It is a splendid system because it places the onus upon an individual of seniority to apply the directive to his own particular situation and carry it out. If a spot check reveals the man has not carried out the general directive in relation to his own case, he leaves himself wide open to be labelled a fool or a knave. I saw plenty of examples myself during the war where chaps found themselves upon the horns of this dilemma and they did not like it one little bit.

Other huge savings of public funds would result from the adoption of such principles as —

1) Expel all government departments from highly rented offices in very congested areas.

2) Put the administration and operation of everything that comes under the Postmaster General on an up-to-date business basis so that the efficiency becomes equal to that of the privately owned companies in America.

3) The Law: British justice and judicial procedure is admired the world over but surely the Law could reform itself or be reformed to make immense savings in the cost to the taxpayer.

4) National Health Service: Pay well the doctors, nurses, and all who personally care for the sick but attack savagely the huge overheads.

5) Aim to reduce over a period of time all form-filling and paper-work in government departments by seventy-five per cent.

Winning An Election

The Labour Party can scarcely deny that their policies mean more regimentation, more little dictators, more officialdom, less personal freedom. All this spells a lot more money, and a lot more money can only mean still more taxation.

The Tory Party policy should be exactly the reverse on all these counts. It is just as simple as that. But how to carry this out? I have discussed this many times with chaps of brain and position and have always received virtually the same reply. And that reply is that these things are easy to promise but verge on the impossible to carry out. To these Doubting Thomases I offer the following story.

Four thousand years ago a king of a small country was in perpetual war with his neighbours and he was always losing battles. After each defeat, his general and their aides gave him clever, clear, and convincing reasons why they had lost yet another battle.

But the old king did not like it at all, so after the next defeat he cut short the explanations of his two chief generals by taking up his sword and slicing off their heads. He then told the No. 2s to take over and a few days later he ordered them to go off and give battle to another of the neighbouring kingdoms.

But they, too, came back defeated, so the old king repeated the process but on a larger scale. After lopping off the heads of the half dozen most senior officers, he got a bit tired so he stopped there and had a round dozen strung up by their thumbs in the hot sun.

A week later there was another border battle and this time his so very newly promoted generals and their army came back jubilant with loot and slaves and the opposing generals in chains. After that the old king never lost a battle.

Everyone knows that the machine of government is extravagant in manpower, and increasingly inefficient as more burdens and complications are piled upon its back by successive acts of Parliament and budgets. But the able and loyal chaps who are units in this vast machine, must work in it as it is. Even a permanent secretary cannot alter fundamentally his slice of the whole. He can make modifications here and there within the framework, but these are mere needles in his portion of the haystack.

The voters have read in their newspapers that successful firms of vast size have not been too proud to call in management and efficiency consultants, and that telling results have been achieved.

I think these even include Shell Oil, ICI, and Courtaulds. Yet these, and other concerns, were super-efficient already by government standards.

I fail to understand why it should need a war with all its suffering and misery to put some cutting of red tape and sense of urgency into the established methods of government departmental procedure. Thirty or forty years ago, the whole idea of "managing" Great Britain was entirely fresh and we were making all the expensive mistakes of experimentation. But with all the modern advances in automation and greater experience each year, we ought to be able to manage this country today with substantially less civil servants – instead of three times the number. Great Britain has grown no larger – just more population. Yet, instead of streamlining the huge machine of government, and gradually reorganizing it from scratch, we have added grossly to it on the same creaky old framework with two major results:

1) A huge additional cost.

2) "The Works" are still more gummed up than they were thirty years ago.

So why should we continue to tolerate this huge and cumbersome organization? Why is it only public expenditure in all its forms, that can afford to spend a couple of hundred million here, and a mere eighty million there, upon projects that subsequently prove worthless or out of date often following five years' delay owing to red tape?

Government and government alone can put in top experienced professionals to start thinking from scratch to find out what is wanted as an end product, and to suggest means of achieving that end by methods universally applied by private industry.

The Prime Minister should follow the example of the old king 4,000 years ago, and then all he has to do is to sit back and watch the economies rolling in. He should have progress reports three times a year, and if the spending departments are not doing their stuff, off with the head of cabinet minister and permanent secretary concerned, and let the No. 2s have a go.

This will not work the first time because I have had a life time of experience of permanent secretaries, and know what I am talking about. So repeat the process with more heads falling and a good deal more of the hanging up by the thumbs.

By this time something will begin to stir because there are a lot of fine and eager chaps, not yet fossilized in the spending departments, who will see this as a miracle of opportunity, and will hang their heads out of the windows of Whitehall to see the next executions taking place, and their own chance of real opportunity as well as promotion for themselves five or eight years earlier than their wildest dreams.

Such a process would inevitably take some years, and nobody can tell what the eventual saving would be, but every thinking person knows that the total would be colossal. My serious guess is that the taxpayer is not getting more than about 80p in the pound value for the colossal sums voted annually to the government spending departments. Yet the citizen and his wife are forced by taxation to make every remaining pound of their net income give 100p net value.

The first government to face up to the problem will certainly earn the support and the votes of the great bulk of the electorate who wish this great national problem to be put to them in simple plain terms, and without vague phrases and ambiguity.

The Tories should make a public announcement that they will, if re-elected with a working majority, take immediate and drastic steps towards a five or seven year goal of giving the voter 100p worth of value for each £ extracted from the nation by direct and indirect taxation.

Instead of making vague promises to reduce taxation wherever possible, the Tories should state clearly that after one year's breathing space they will take at least 2p off the standard rate of tax every year of the succeeding four years. And still balance the budget. They would also make annual tax reductions in those items in daily use or consumption which at present bear exorbitant tax burdens. It would drive the promise home to voters, both men and women, if these scheduled tax reductions were shown in actual figures. A dated promise of purchase tax reductions should also be made.

The Common Market

I have already stated my view that the present system of government has run its course and that an alternative should be worked out for the eventual future. Tennyson wrote: "Our little systems have their day. They have their day and cease to be."

These last few years of controversy over the pro's and cons of England joining the Common Market is the best possible example of how little equipped the voter is to make any solid assessment at all, let alone foresee which course will be proved in future years to have been the right one.

I was among those for whom it was part of my daily job to weigh up this proposal, both for and against. Aveling-Barford's old established goodwill and distribution arrangements throughout Europe are of very major importance so we were vitally concerned from the outset. Aveling-Barford yes – but England?? Knowing this, two newspaper proprietor acquaintances, approached me within a few weeks of each other requesting my views, one saying that this invitation was going only to four or five other chaps whom he named.

I would like to have said yes or no and given overwhelming reasons in concise form, but I could not do this, for the very simple reason that I did not know myself. This is equally true today – I still do not know.

That is bad enough, but worse is now to follow.

I made one clear-cut discovery as a result of all the headaches of thought: on small facets upon which I had special knowledge, the spokesmen on either side were often quite wrong in what purported to be statements of fact. Meanwhile, I was discovering that lots of other chaps were saying that the politicians' spokesmen were being primed with honest opinions – but opinions loaded up as fact.

The trouble is that a clever man often falls into the pitfall of pre-judging an issue at an early stage and most of his subsequent thinking and research are directed to additional arguments towards the one side only.

The politicians are not much help. Mr. Wilson was heartily in favour of the Common Market when in power, but when defeated he executed a complete turnabout upon a laughably thin excuse. Mr. Heath nailed his flag to the mast so long ago that it has been, most obviously, the prime call upon his time since he came to power.

I say that nobody, and no group of so-called experts can foretell whether or not the next generation will be happy or sad, but one thing is clear – once we are finally in the Common Market it is the duty of all citizens to do their damndest to make a success of it, each in our own sphere.

Let us forget present politics and personalities. We owe that to succeeding generations.

Industrial Relations

During the run-up to the last General Election it was clear to all that Industrial Relations remained the most urgent and the most important problem of any facing the new Government. There was nothing new or unexpected. My speech to shareholders, reprinted earlier, could be said again today. All we have had since is a diarrhoea of words but a constipation of actions.

Mr. Heath has, on several occasions, exhorted the managements of industry to take this opportunity to buy the latest machinery and equipment in order to put themselves in the best possible position to deal with the flood of orders that he, Mr. Heath, confidently expects. But his remarks are no more than rhetoric and wishful thinking, as well as underlining that his preoccupation with the Common Market has left him out of touch with industrial problems at home.

What is the use of firms buying new machinery to increase production per man when it is obvious that the present type of shop steward will call a wildcat strike under the banner of "No Redundancies"? In other words, if a new machine could be easily operated by one man and the present machine requires two men to operate it, the Unions will insist that two men should be employed to operate the new machine. Unless and until managements have full power to organize and manage their labour force as they think best and in the interest of maximum production and competitive costs, it would indeed be wrong for the shareholders' money to be wasted. I have never heard of a case where the management have broken a fully debated and carefully drawn up, written and signed three year agreement, by repudiating it within one year, yet this has happened so frequently on the labour side that it is taken as a matter of course.

Optimum production per man reduces costs, prices to the consumer at home and increases export trade so that everyone benefits and more labour force is required, and it is obvious that this brings higher wages.

Then there is the all-important matter of social benefits. For instance, after the miners' strike in the early part of this year, their leaders boasted that they could have lasted out for twelve months if necessary. This of course is almost solely due to social benefits, etc., paid to the strikers for the maintenance of their wives and children, but the strikers themselves benefit equally. In other words, the Tory government have continued to make striking very easy at national expense without any regard to all the harm and loss to almost everybody else. The benefits to strikers should be strictly limited to what is actually legally due to them as a result of their Social Security contributions. This should have been top priority directly after the election; a simple firm action removing this absurdity as soon as the Tories came into power would have been of far more benefit than the whole of the Industrial Relations Bill, which could have followed later.

There is, of course, a great difference between a sudden wildcat strike and a properly organized official strike by the Unions concerned, and this difference should be clearly catered for in payments from the public purse.

As I write this, I see that at long last our legislators are looking into this matter. Why so dilatory? Or so lofty as to be out of touch with the affairs of ordinary folk? Meanwhile, they have been responsible for much further inflation.

I am sure that almost all decent citizens who follow this national problem on the TV and radio, and in newspapers, will agree with me that those of our fellow citizens, men and women, we should cater for fully are those who become redundant through no fault of their own. This of course is covered by recent legislation but perhaps we should go even further. I cannot understand why we should mollycoddle from the public purse the workshy, the bad timekeepers and careless workers, whose employment should be terminated unless they pull up their socks and give an honest day's work for an honest day's pay.

Then there is the major inequality that the national purse pours out vast sums to help the strikers but does nothing whatever for the other partner in industry, namely shareholders who today mainly consist of the man in the street with very small savings. (Some public companies point out that their individual share-holders have an average holding of £250 apiece.) Take as a single example, which is duplicated throughout every branch of industry, the case of that vast combine BLMC whose total profits dropped from about forty million pounds to almost nothing in one year, obviously due almost entirely to labour troubles. The public purse is the largest individual loser because it loses about twenty million pounds in corporation profits tax – the business itself and its shareholders lose the remainder.

In most companies, the small shareholder (under £300 either direct or through Unit Trusts, Pension Funds, etc., etc.) out-number, often vastly, the striking operatives. Surely they have a greater right to any compensation from the national purse? The man in the street sees the value of his hard-earned savings taking a nosedive and ruefully feels that over all the years he ought to have put £2 a week on the pools instead!

Our old friend, commonsense, tells us that it is better to let all sections of industry stand on their own feet. The will to survive is a most potent spur. But why spend some of the proceeds of taxation, levied upon each and all of us, to subsidize one section against another?

Why does not Mr. Heath or Mr. Carr make the following fundamental fact clear to the nation as a whole? The march of progress over the last two hundred years, and the further con-gestion of population into the large towns, which has resulted in enormous benefits to the living standards of the masses has equally pinpointed the solid fact that today even quite small sections of the total population can, and do, enormously disrupt the daily lives and even livelihood of the nation as a whole.

I give the following example of what I mean, Rowney Priory in Hertfordshire (my country home which I sold about a year ago for obvious reasons) has been in bygone years both an Abbey and a Priory. It is clear that in those far-off days the Abbey, surrounded by its 500 acres, was self supporting and some of the old evidence of this still exists. It had its own wells and a spring for water. It had its own cows for milk, its own bullocks for meat, and its own poultry of all kinds. The small lake was stocked with edible fish, and fresh water from the spring flowed through it. They made their own tallow candles for light from the residue of the animals. For heating, they had the wood from the older trees coupled with peat from some of the hard dry ground. They made their own simple wines from the fermentation of garden produce, as others did in those days.

For the little money they needed, the monks and later the nuns produced articles of great beauty, principally religious, such as chalices, beautifully chased in silver, and tapestries, which were sold.

This is an example of how hundreds of self-contained communities lived several centuries ago. The population was much less and each village was self-supporting in a parallel way. At Rowney Priory even twenty years ago, any occupier foreseeing trouble could have made his family and his small community independent of outside supplies.

Today the wheel has turned with so much progress that it is virtually impossible for any individual to be self-sufficient and each one of us is dependent upon others for the smooth progress of our daily routine.

Any government should be there for the benefit of the nation as a whole and it has the power to prevent any single section using the results of the march of progress to obtain large pay rises, or other benefits, at the expense of everybody else.

Mr. Heath and his colleagues have stressed on several occasions their responsibilities to the nation as a whole without fear or favour. We have heard the words – now let us see the action.

Payments towards Nationalized Services

It is common experience and knowledge that something for nothing is often so little appreciated that it is derided. During the last twenty years the rise in wages and weekly salaries has far outstripped the increase in the cost of living, but National Health contributions represent only a small portion of the total cost of the Health Scheme. My suggestion is that each patient should pay something, say 40p, at the surgery before seeing the doctor (prevent paperwork).

The advantages are so obvious. The backbone of England, the better type of weekly wage earner, is independent minded. He would be paying say one quarter or one fifth of the doctor's fee. The visits of the malingerers and hypochondriacs would be much reduced, thus freeing the doctor to attend to cases of genuine illness. The status of the doctor (once so high) would receive much-needed improvement, and there would be some relief on the national purse.

The same solutions largely apply to Education and Child Welfare. Why should a couple who are deprived of children, to their sorrow, have to pay for others whom they cannot fail to envy? Women, in particular, desperately hope for the joys of motherhood. Why should not they pay say twenty per cent or twenty five per cent towards the cost of their own baby?

Quite apart from the money, England is overpopulated already. If a couple do not want a baby sufficiently to pay towards its birth and doctoring, then they should not add to the population. Some couples make almost a living out of having a huge family and then dumping the cost of it all on the State. Equally, why should not parents make a contribution towards Education?

We give each citizen a vote, so that he or she is an equal citizen with everybody else. Let us also raise his sense of personal independence instead of letting some Trade Unions treat them like blocks of nitwits to be ordered here and there. Mass voting (with punishment for disobedience) and no secret ballot.

The measures I suggest will help the man-in-the-street to retrieve his individuality.

CHAPTER ELEVEN

ANECDOTES, FUN, PEOPLE OF ACHIEVEMENT
(together with the author's views on more weighty matters)

Bentley Racing Cars

When the history of the motor car comes to be written, the memory and reputation of W. O. Bentley will rank high as a pioneer designer of cars that gave as much sheer delight to the dedicated driver as a chinchilla coat plus a diamond necklace would give to a woman.

For about forty years it has been every young motorist's dream to drive a Bentley, and all the prettiest girls have equally liked to be seen in them. And why not? It is no sin to hope to make other females a trifle envious. It is, in fact, an international female pastime, or otherwise the female sex would wear their clothes until they are threadbare, like men do. And then the fashion industry would go completely *phut*!

But Bentley cars also meant as much to a man of almost any age. It made an older man feel younger, and more vigorous, to sit at the wheel of this gorgeous mechanical animal – so strong, so safe, with such fierce acceleration and such strong brakes. You could take a calculated risk with a Bentley that would be foolhardy with lesser cars. Naturally, I am excluding risks that could conceivably involve anyone but yourself.

In order to achieve and maintain this supremacy competition motor racing was essential. And so the Bentley Boys came into being.

I was not really close to it all until the late Babe Barnato, a really lovable chap of great wealth, came right into the picture by buying a large interest in the Bentley company. A superb driver himself, he led the Bentley racing team, aided and supported by other young rich chaps who had the nerve, stamina, and skill to drive these wonderful chassis with racing bodies to victory all over Europe. Precisely the same could be said of another friend, the late Tim Birkin (Sir Timothy Birkin, Bart.), whose fortune, I believe, came from Nottingham lace, and who equalled Babe in the courage and skills that are the make-up of an international racing driver.

I longed and thirsted to be even a dogsbody in the company of these wonderful drivers, who also included Clive and Jack Dunfee and several other friends of mine.

They allowed me to train and practise for a few months, so that I learned how to do a skid turn round a hairpin bend, how to tackle ice and snow on a road safely, but at twice the speed that is safe for ordinary motorists.

By the courtesy of what was then the London General Omnibus Company we are allowed to try our hand on the Chiswick "oiler". This was – and, I believe, still is – a concreted area with about an inch of old sump oil from London's buses poured over it. The sides were largely lined with pieces of old tyres also from the buses, and the vehicles were the chassis of discarded buses with a bit of planking for a seat, also festooned with lengths of old tyres, so that when you ran into the side, they cushioned the collision. There was a prescribed "course" and every trainee London bus driver in those days had to pass a test before qualifying to drive a LGOC bus.

We, of course, were meat and drink to these fine chaps, and to any bus staff who had a right to be there during the occasional two hour spells when we were permitted to chance our arm with their vehicles. To them, we were as good as free seats to the London Palladium variety shows or the opening day of Bertram Mills' Circus. Pipes in mouth, they put their elbows on the barrier and gave us the best of Cockney encouragement tempered, of course, with the wrong advice, so that some of us never did make the prescribed "course".

But motor racing was not for me. I could excuse myself by saying that I had neither the time nor the money. Both were true. It is equally true that I lacked the very quick reflexes which are an essential and primary attribute for this particular sport. I recognized this myself, and so my motor-racing career finished before it had begun.

Lord Castlerosse and the "Great Fight"

During the late 'twenties there was billed at the Albert Hall one of the greatest fights of all time. Carpentier, the Frenchman, who was then the greatest boxer in the world, was to fight Bombardier Billy Wells, the British champion.

I had been trained to box, both at my preparatory school and at Rugby, and continued it in the army in the First World War before I was shipped to France. But the price of even back row tickets for this great fight was well beyond my purse.

This was a pity, because I could see the difference between a powerful short and hurting jab and a round armer to the face – which latter blow always brought roars of applause from those "sportsmen" who could afford twenty guineas for a ticket, £1 for a cigar and 2s. for a clove carnation, but who didn't really know a thing about the noble art of boxing. However, fortune favoured me.

A couple of days before the fight Valentine (Viscount) Castlerosse of Express Newspapers telephoned me to ask if I would like to accompany him and Freddie Lonsdale, the playwright, to the fight in the ringside seats allocated to the newspaper group.

Valentine, who was probably the most popular newspaper columnist of that time, adored a little club off St. James's Street named the Orleans. After about twenty minutes discussion with both the chef and the head waiter, it was agreed that the delicious simple dinner which he had ordered the previous day would just about suffice for our needs. Castlerosse really understood his food, and his huge belly was evidence that he also enjoyed it.

In due course the three of us were on our way in a taxi to the Albert Hall, bowling along the road inside the park that runs parallel with Knightsbridge. As we neared the Albert Hall, the park gates were closed, as was the custom after dark.

"Valentine," said Freddie, "why are the park gates closed?"

Valentine: "Because of the things boys and girls might do to each other after dark in the park, you chump."

Freddie: "Well, they may make it uncomfortable, but they'll never make it unpopular!"

So convulsed was I at this riposte that I might well have fallen out of the taxi if Valentine's huge bulk and his huge cigar had not held me prisoner.

Before we left the taxi I pinned on to my lapel a large card on which was prominently printed "Express Newspapers Sports Editor". In the ten minute interval between the end of the previous bout and the start of the main one, I stood up with great glee and turned round hoping that some of my friends would see me in the ringside seat and be convulsed with jealousy. Valentine gave such a furious tug at my coat that I lost my balance.

"You bloody fool, there are scores of reporters here in the seats behind us. You aren't a sports editor of Express Newspapers, whatever else you may think you are. Chaps can read the printing on that card for about five rows back."

The Bombardier was a huge chap compared to the Frenchman, and about three stone heavier, but Carpentier finished the fight in a flash. A leap—both feet off the floor. Most unorthodox. The straight left of a Greek god and a right jab that would have felled an elephant. The fight was over.

We had not brought a hunting flask of brandy with us. Both my companions were too upstage for my common habits. But those within earshot (about ten feet even in that noisy scuffle towards the exit) heard, for free, with much enjoyment, my two companions arguing as to whether we should go back to the Orleans Club to finish our dinner or not—or whether the chef had already eaten it up himself or taken it home to his starving wife and children.

My portly host was a striking figure, especially in his opera cloak and his gleaming white waistcoat (laundered daily) with his dinner jacket. Moreover, he was well known to the *canaille* who crowded around to see the mighty drive off in their Rolls-Royces.

Our Rolls was a taxi which appeared like lightning, although we were right at the back of the queue. Valentine rattled a couple of halfcrowns in his hand, but that was nothing. It was his grand appearance and manner that wooed the cabbie.

Tennis against Henri Cochet

In the mid 'twenties, I once found myself in the truly awesome position of discovering that my opponent in a tennis competition was none other than Henri Cochet, one of the world's greatest singles players, who indeed became world champion about a couple of years later.

I have always loved the game and been a very keen performer. For instance, after a long day's work, I used to go to a covered and flood-lighted court in Hill Road, St. John's Wood, which was then a sort of private club, and we each had a locker and could book the court in advance.

Here I would practise assiduously with the pros or try to defeat my equally rabbity friends and acquaintances. Here also the great W. T. Tilden used to practise regularly before the opening of the leading British open championships, culminating in the All England Championships at Wimbledon.

Tilden, the nicest of chaps, would play a friendly set against other ranking players. But on perhaps half a dozen occasions his opponent was either late or telephoned to apologize for his absence, and I was there in the little spectators' gallery all eager to study how the great Tilden made the deep ground shots for which he was so famous and for which he continues to be remembered in tennis history. He had to have someone on the other side of the net, if only to throw the balls back to his side.

I obliged very willingly, but, of course, I never returned one of his cannon-ball services unless the ball happened to hit my racket, which I flailed around, hoping for the best. He was very kind and coached me a bit and gave most excellent advice, but it was very clear that his unspoken thoughts were that I was a rabbit at the game and would always remain one – however much I practised.

Having explained my tennis "ranking", I turn back to Henri Cochet. In France, as in England, annual open tournaments were held at a few of the top ranking clubs, usually on the Riviera in the very early spring and elsewhere in the summer. On this particular occasion I had entered one in Brittany in the summer, and had scraped through two rounds against a couple of "six and out" carefree bashers, like myself, when I read on the board to my utter dismay that my next opponent was Henri Cochet, who was joining the tournament in the third round. (All the profits were going to charities in Brittany, and Cochet, of course, was the great "draw" for the gate money.)

I was introduced to him while we sat waiting for the previous match to finish. He was smiling and charming, but we couldn't converse because his English was almost as non-existent as my French. He was small, neat, and rather tubby then, while I was, and am, huge and clumsy. And I was sweating with stage-fright, because all reserved seats and even standing room had become packed.

I served first and double-faulted three times out of sheer nerves. The upshot of it all was that Cochet gave me one game in each of the two sets (three set matches) so cleverly that I was certain that nobody but Brugnon, his doubles partner, knew that he was doing it carefully and deliberately. He just placed some of his shots less than a foot outside the court, and not a smile on his face – just resigned Gallic shrugs.

I taxed him with it over an iced beer afterwards. He shrugged it off with a charming smile and a wink which the London news-paper reporter who was interpreting could not see.

A couple of days afterwards the late Lord Kemsley (whom I was to know well in later years) buttonholed me to show me some small cuttings from the sports pages of London dailies. *The Times* noted: "Barford battled gamely and took a game in each set against Henri Cochet, that wonderful master, whose courtcraft is sheer delight to watch."

If Cochet had been out to win every point, I might have got two points in the match – not two games!

My Pheasant Shoot

Owing to trouble in my left eye, I gave up pheasant and partridge shooting on my estate a number of years ago, but until very recently I kept the shoot going to give pleasure and exercise to my family and close friends.

A couple of shooting seasons ago I joined my friend of about twenty years' standing, Mr. Reginald Maudling, who is just as simple and friendly to my estate workers and other regular beaters as he was when I first met him as a PPS, just one step up from back-bencher in the House of Commons.

Reggie had not drawn a good place, but was standing correctly behind the numbered stick at the rear of my small lake and beside a large teak garden seat (always a bit off-putting). A few pheasants got up five or six hundred yards away, and it was downwind, so they were flying flat out and swerving and rising as they saw the line of guns. One strong old cock that had obviously survived a previous season or two was heading straight overhead when he spied Maudling, his loader, and the portly squire (myself).

Though at forty miles an hour he had time to make a sharp vertical bank and swerve at the same time – I judged him to be still within range. I was all set to say "Bad luck, Reggie", but his face tightened, he raised his gun, swung easily, quickly, and accurately, squeezed the trigger – and the gallant old cock came hurtling down five yards behind us.

And then precisely the same thing happened again, and a second bird landed within a yard of the first. Incredibly, it happened a third time, scarcely giving Maudling time to reload. This was a case for very real congratulation and I gave it unstintingly.

"Three out of three of most difficult birds – and all right in the beak," said I.

"Hold hard, Edward," said Reggie, "It was four out of four."

Mr. Featherstone, one of my loyal friends from Grantham who came down on shooting days, had been crouching with his dog in the little spinney a few yards behind us, and within half a minute had laid the four birds at our feet.

This, of course, was a pheasant-shooting feat of the highest order and the huge boyish grin on the Maudling face made my day. I think it made his, too, as the news spread among all those who were enjoying a pleasant day's sport.

An equally popular guest with all was my friend, Sir Ian Orr-Ewing (now Lord-Orr Ewing). A fine sportsman in every way, if ever there was one.

Another fine neighbour was Prince Frederick of Prussia, whose charming gentle modesty made it hard to realize that he was the grandson of the German Kaiser. All children adored him because he adored all children and showed it. His untimely death was a sad blow to us.

Many other friends, of course, were my shooting guests over a period of nearly twenty years – locals, Londoners, and from elsewhere, or other countries. I have narrated the Maudling incident because he is deservedly so prominent in the Tory Government and the names of the other two came naturally to my mind.

The best shot who ever came to my estate was the late Hugh McCorquodale, husband of Barbara Cartland, the authoress. The ease and grace with which he killed his birds was sheer joy to watch. He was considered one of the dozen best pheasant shots in England.

Debutante Parties of Yester-year

Until debutante parties started again after the war, the role of the young male guest was pretty clearly defined. As in pheasant shooting, the code of conduct and behaviour was unwritten but clear and concise, and understood by all who took a role in such pleasantly expensive activities.

For those who were neither nobly nor even gently born, but who had acquired wealth in just one or two generations, the objective was not merely to keep up with the Joneses — but to beat them to it good and proper, with suitable gossip-writer publicity. No harm in such an aim, provided the father of the darling deb does not suffer a heart attack when his secretary tots up the bills and places them demurely before him.

Before the war, the titular head of most important families had a large London house, known as their town house, and often occupied in part for only a very few months of the year. But the wretched chap was sternly warned and reminded well in advance by his consort and others that it was his duty and pleasure to have preparations made to open up the house completely for the ensuing debutante season.

He was the titular head of the clan, so even nieces and step-nieces must be catered for. And he must be seen by all to be there himself for at least part of the London season, and particularly for the ball-dance (I think I invented this word), to be held in his town house.

The mother asked, or bullied, relations and friends to give dinner parties for the ball-dance, and sent to each of them a list of suitable girls and young men to invite.

And now we come to the unwritten rules as they affected the young chaps such as myself. At the dinner party you noted the face of your hostess and of the two girls on both sides. Luckily you probably knew them already, which made the whole operation easier.

The point is that at the ball-dance it was your duty to beg the pleasure of a dance with five females, to wit your dinner-hostess (who always gently refused) and the two girls nearest you at dinner on both sides – after that, you could do what you liked, within the bounds of decorum.

Sometimes these elegant affairs did not go with the swing that they deserved after all the hard work and effort that had been expended upon them. And decorum was served if young and old started to slink off about 1 a.m.

If one was lucky enough to have a couple of quid in one's trouser pocket, one begged a delicious little piece of stuff (that was a phrase then) to accompany you to the Embassy for an hour or so. The Embassy in Bond Street then was no relation to the present one, except that it had the same name and was in roughly the same premises.

I apologize freely if I am in error, but the pre-war Embassy Club was most extremely exclusive – even more so than such men's clubs as White's and Buck's are today. Louis, the great restaurateur, knew all the members by name and held the first banquette table on the left firmly empty if he had received a message that the Prince of Wales might appear. Another regular was Viscount Castlerosse, who sometimes had the pleasure of the charming and beautiful company of the lady who is now Mrs. Ralph Hubbard of Goodwood racecourse fame.

The great Ambrose and his band were the sole entertainment and nothing more could possibly have been needed – service and food of a quality unsurpassed anywhere in any country. So sometimes I wound up in the early morning at the Embassy.

Perhaps three or four couples would arrange at the ball-dance to meet again at the Embassy, and did so. It was pretty late by then and thoughts of nine o'clock at the office would flick uneasily through male minds. Some couples went off earlier than others, and by pure mischance would forget to leave an estimated share of the bill – so that the last couple left at the table got the bill for the lot.

That most entertaining and charming woman, Barbara Cartland, the novelist and ardent crusader for such charities and causes as touch her heart, was a deb at that time, and she solved the problem for all the other debs and their escorts.

It was very simple – place an empty glass in the middle of the table and let every man put so much money into it. There was then always enough to pay the bill at the end.

The Hansom Cab Race

I have not seen a Hansom cab in London for several years but like King Charles II they took an unconscionable time dying, though in Central Park New York there were a half a dozen or so even two or three years ago. They provided a leisurely, romantic ride that takes a lot of beating. Both cabbie and his horse knew that speed of arrival was the greatest error and the slower the trot the greater the tip. This is an unfair remark because the Cockney cabbie enjoyed to the full all that he saw and heard in the close and intimate confines of the Hansom cab. There is nothing today comparable and more's the pity.

Fearing the end of the Hansom cab was near, a few members of the St. James's Street clubs decided to hold a "Farewell to the London Hansom Cabby", which was to take the form of a timed race. The course was plotted down St. James's Street, left along Pall Mall, up Lower Regent Street, round Piccadilly Circus and into Soho to the winning post, a well known night club. It was all carefully worked out weeks in advance and details of the plan were submitted to the police, who gave their assent to this "prank", subject to certain conditions, which were rigidly adhered to by all concerned.

The rules included not more than twelve cabs in the race with two "fares" in each. The cabs to start in pairs at three-minute intervals, and stewards with stop-watches to be on duty to check the times accurately.

The course was tested several times, so everybody had some idea of what the winning time might be, and "zero" hour was midnight, to minimize traffic holdups.

For two weeks beforehand, the "fares" were permitted to recompense the cabbies for putting the competing horses on light duty, with plenty of oats. The word got round quickly and the cabbies co-operated splendidly. It was the Cabbies' Derby and each one with a good youngish horse competed to find an "owner". The owners took as much care in selecting their "hoss and cabby"

134

as they would when buying thoroughbreds at the Newmarket sales – and never forget that Papyrus was pulling a cab before he was bought by a tenant farmer near Huntingdon and went on to win the Derby, becoming one of the great stallions of that age.

At the draw I was pleased to find myself teamed with a good friend David (the Earl of) Northesk, so we selected a cabby with a fine young cob that was surefooted and eager and pulled well on our trial run. His owner and driver was just the right old fashioned type, with twenty-five years of experience, and a bellow that would startle any human out of his path.

We thought nobody knew about our frolic, but three or four days before the race paragraphs appeared in the London evening newspapers, naming the cabbies and their horses, plus some of the passengers. Experienced police guessed that quite a lot of Londoners might turn up on the pavements to laugh, cheer, or give good-hearted derisory shouts of encouragement or disdain.

David Northesk and I had drawn last place at the start and it was soon obvious that this was an advantage because the onlookers by this time were shooing the other traffic out of our path to give the cabbies a clearer run. Old George, our cabby, was bellowing and so were we, our cob was going splendidly and his tail was so taut that it was almost in the cab with us. David had the stop-watch and was yelling with glee as we rounded Piccadilly Circus. A few hundred yards only from the night club an onlooker must have frightened our pony for he swerved on to the pavement and we crashed into a lamp-post. All horsey folk know that when a frightened horse is down in harness and kicking around madly, the correct procedure is for someone to sit firmly on his head and try to keep there while others loosen the harness and get him out of the shafts before he damages himself. This I endeavoured to do – somewhat inexpertly as I had never done it before (or since). The upshot of it all was that about ten minutes later the pony was on his feet again with no obvious signs of hurt but the cabby and his two fares, sweaty and dishevelled, were a sorry sight.

But then insult added to our injury. A plain-clothes detective and two constables arrested us (to the delight of some of the crowd). We protested, which was a silly thing to do. So off we were marched at the head of quite a procession to the nearest police station, where statements were taken from all concerned and we were made vaguely aware of what we might be charged with – drunk and disorderly, obstruction to traffic, and cruelty to a horse.

By now it was about 3 a.m. and David and I were put in a cell. The police were very fair and courteous. They gave us hot soup and agreed that we could phone a lawyer. So we phoned George Gordon, founder of Gordon Dadds & Co. He woke smartly and within about forty-five minutes was with us bearing a large basket containing food he had rifled from his own kitchen, plus hock and beer. He was certainly a friend in need, for this was a Saturday night and we should have to spend two nights in the cells, though we might be allowed out during the day, before appearing before Mr. Mead the Metropolitan magistrate on the Monday.

Still it wasn't so bad after all. Naturally everybody had been very abstemious before the race so that the police doctor had found no sign of drunkenness. The magistrate ruled that the police had acted correctly, though perhaps rather hastily and we were discharged without a stain on our characters.

How to Lose Money

I have had six or seven adventures in business – or calculated gambles, of which two have been failures.

In 1923, when I was nearly 25, my father died leaving practically no money. My mother had only £200 a year of her own. My teenage sister was "finishing" in Paris. It wasn't rags to riches in reverse because there never had been great riches anyway, but it was the sort of almighty shock that either makes or breaks you. Solid financial security died with my father. From now on I realized I was on my own, and with family responsibilities which I felt it was my duty, as well as my wish, to undertake.

My first failure was an investment which I made in a goldmine near Pumpsaint in Wales which had been worked by the Romans after they had conquered England.

In about 1937, the promoters issued a very private prospectus under the name Roman Deep. This prospectus was so private and so limited in its circulation that I cannot think how I was invited. Several members of the Royal Household were already "in", plus the odd cabinet minister or two. Roman Deep had the cachet of supplying British gold for royal wedding rings from monarch downwards.

Apparently the mine had been worked in a desultory fashion from time to time ever since those far-off days, but now investigation by qualified goldmining experts suggested that if capital were raised the mine could be modernized and greatly extended to work profitably to the benefit of all concerned, particularly the under-employed Welsh coalminers.

I do not remember how or why I was invited to join such a small upper-crust group, but I had just floated Aveling-Barford so Lloyds Bank were happy to loan me money.

I went into this gamble much too heavily, and it took only a couple of years for me to lose every penny.

Precisely the same thing happened with the Jules Hotel in Jermyn Street, and at the same time. Three or four of us bought it for a song in 1937 after Monsieur Jules had died. I remember well the small price we paid for the whole shooting match – the hotel and everything in it, including large reserves of cutlery and linen.

Could we go wrong? It appeared impossible, but we succeeded in achieving the impossible.

I was merely the largest shareholder, or nearly so: I had nothing to do with the management. The war clouds were already gathering and Duff Cooper, then Minister of War, had asked me to become a member of what was then called the Tank Board, and so my interest in the Jules Hotel investment largely vanished. But there were still requests almost quarterly for me as principal proprietor to put up more cash to preserve my own asset and "keep the ship afloat".

I asked Aveling-Barford's accountants, Price Waterhouse, to send one or two of their lads along to have a look at the books and accounts. Their short written and verbal report was terrible – but terse, clear, and understandable, too – so the late Lord Brocket and I as principal proprietors decided to "close the shop".

Before doing so, we delved into our pockets and paid off in full all the small creditors and small suppliers – the worthy people who had supplied us with goods. Nobody went bankrupt or was not paid for goods already supplied. All wages and salaries due were paid by us.

Only after all this did we give instructions for the necessary machinery to be put in motion, namely that the company could not pay its debts. A receiver was appointed so that the whole enterprise went bust. Every pound and every penny was lost by those who had risked so much, or so little.

A few months later, Jules Hotel and all its contents were leased by the United States Government for an officer's club, and at a rent which made my hair stand on end.

The Americans did a fine job on the place. They put in many more bathrooms and spruced up the whole building. I think the Americans started this game of almost every double room having a bathroom or shower, plus bidet.

After the Second World War, Jules Hotel in Jermyn Street, London, W.1, was no longer needed by the Americans, and was put on sale for the second time since the death of Monsieur Jules; and it has been sold and re-sold since.

It would appear that had I hung on to it (at practically no cost in view of Inland Revenue Tax losses), I, as principal shareholder, would today have increased the value of my investment by about forty or fifty times, instead of losing it all.

In other words, today's valuation for the whole caboodle is probably forty to fifty times what we bought it for in 1937 after making full allowance for money spent on it after the United States Government surrendered their lease. But that is life. It is better to be a good loser than a good winner.

These two speculations taught me a very worthwhile lesson. The old adage, "every man to his last", is just as true today as 100 years ago.

If my reader has accumulated savings over a number of years in a form of business in which he is confident of making a success by branching out on his own, don't go risking your hard-earned savings in some speculation you know bloody well nothing about. Some of us have learned by experience not to emulate the cow to whom "the grass is always greener on the other side of the fence".

In other words, look before you leap into pastures new.

It is natural that in newspapers you read only of the successful ones. You can be sure that each one had a very long hard look before he or she "leapt".

People I Have Known

WE DO not all reach the dizzy heights which cause head waiters to genuflect at the very sight of us.

But we're not all failures, either. Not for us the common rut which gives us the title of "solid citizen, shrewd, and successful", "good brain and balance", "fine chap for this constituency next time", "openhanded in charities and good work, but not to be fooled so do not try that on".

Deep is our admiration for these chaps, and but for them the world would stop going round, or at least turn more slowly. But we do not envy them. For us, the spice and fun, the joys, worries, and disappointments come from tilting our lance at something we know we can never achieve; from feeling we are right. And so we fight people we could never hope to beat.

We hold views that belonged to someone in the classics – we do not know who, because of defects in our education. But we know that many thousands of years ago some old character ran a country better than our rulers today – so we belong to no political party.

Yet we have got by. Sometimes rich, sometimes poor, sometimes envious, too.

Some seem happier who are not even lance-corporals of industry. Some seem less happy who have climbed the dizzy heights and are (newly created) belted Earls with villas, yachts, sparklers, and chinchilla pyjamas. So what is it all about?

I have been very lucky in people I have met who were or are influential in widely differing spheres.

I will start in the distant past with personalities who were at their peak long before most of my readers were even a gleam in their father's eyes.

The days of confiscation by the Inland Revenue of over ninety per cent of any gross income over a rather moderate figure (having regard to roaring inflation), did not arrive until the Second World War. In the mid and late twenties, a man or woman with a largish income, earned or unearned, could keep nearly half of it, and the pound then purchased about six times what it does in 1972.

So those Englishmen who could afford to have their shirts made for them by hand in the West End of London were apt to be greeted by such shirtmakers as the great Mr. Izod, then of Conduit Street, with some such remark as: "You have chosen the patterns, sir, so I shall make you half a dozen of each, or maybe a dozen would be more convenient for you and your valet?"

Freddie Curtis, a founder of Hawes & Curtis, then in Jermyn Street, changed all that dramatically. He and his staff hoped for big orders but smiled just as warmly if poor chaps like me ordered only three evening shirts and three day shirts, say twice a year.

Then he went one better — a great deal better.

The first sign of old age on a man's shirt is usually fraying at the cuff, or a stain on one cuff that won't wash out. When wearing an evening shirt and dinner jacket, a chap may be so enthralled by his female companion that he spills some claret down his shirtfront, and maybe it's a new one. The attitude of Freddie's competitors was "Order some more shirts, sir".

Freddie's attitude was: "Bring the damaged shirts back to us, and we will tell you whether there is enough life left in the rest of the shirt to warrant the cost of putting in a new piece, so that your shirt can return to normal service."

In the case of coloured collar-attached shirts, he would advise that his workroom could take a piece out of the tail to make a replacement matching collar, and replace the missing piece of tail with the nearest match the workroom had in stock.

Freddie used to say: "After all, only your girlfriend and your laundry sees the tail of your shirt. And the laundry is impersonal and doesn't count."

One day I was looking at shirt patterns and discussing them with one of Freddie's bright assistants, when the door burst open because a chap was barging in with his arms more or less full of dirty shirts. He was the Prince of Wales (now the Duke of Windsor), and he dumped the load of shirts on the counter next to me. The assistant excused himself politely to me, bowed to the Prince and dashed off to fetch Freddie from his little office.

I want to make it quite clear that the Prince of Wales did not know me by name, but it was clear that he knew me fairly well by sight because he chatted away without asking me to remind him of my name.

But directly Freddie appeared, he leant across the counter and asked Freddie, that experienced diplomatic shirtmaker, for my name, and Freddie obviously told the Prince of Wales in a couple of sentences all that was necessary.

After I had selected my patterns, I was drawn into their careful discussion. Two or three of the Prince's favourite shirts were ruthlessly discarded by Freddie, who even took them outside the shop door to hold them up to the light to show the wear, to prove that they must be scrapped.

His Royal Highness the Prince of Wales, heir to the throne of England, the future Emperor of India, King of all the British Empire, was then the most important young man in the world. But he took just as much trouble over his part-worn shirts of favourite patterns as I did—the impecunious and insignificant young Barford!

Each of us must always bear in mind that probably three-quarters of the men and women of outstanding achievement are totally unknown to us, the general public.

Often they deliberately shun any form of publicity; often their work and lives do not attract mention in newspapers or periodicals or on television. But if you want free publicity, then go and commit a murder or some other 'orrible crime! Or go kick a policeman in the face in Grosvenor Square. You'll get plenty of it then, probably much more than you bargained for.

The entertainment world, politics, big business, huge wealth, a high-ranking inherited title, are a few examples of careers which attract publicity for the successful, and this is immensely enhanced by the skilful exercise of the art of public relations.

One of the best and most painstaking doctors I have come across is a National Health doctor at Puckeridge who would be furious if I mentioned his name. But we've all heard plenty about Dr. Christiaan Barnard haven't we? The heads of our great colleges and our universities carry heavy responsibility. We know Lord Butler is one, but can you put a name to even a few of the others? The situation is so obvious that no elaboration is necessary.

Generally speaking, I have found that persons of achievement or notoriety refer to their ancestry in two entirely opposite ways.

Those in the first think up for themselves an aristocratic and romantic ancestry, and by plenty of repetition and name-dropping hope that their social friends and acquaintances believe them. At any rate, their friends are probably kind enough not to laugh outright into the social climber's face. That's enough about them.

The others are, of course, a much more interesting and amusing study. Churchill had plenty of them around him. That doughty warrior would never let himself be beaten on any score, so he played down his aristocratic ancestry and emphasized that all he could manage to get as a mounted reporter in the Boer War was about £2 a week, and sometimes he had to pay for his forage and horse-grooming.

One of the best stories about this second group was one old Gordon Selfridge was fond of telling about himself. I ought to know, because he offered me the job of being one of his personal assistants and his son Gordon Selfridge junior is godfather to my eldest child.

At a very tender age young Selfridge got a job in the lower basement of the huge Marshall Field Store in Chicago. Into this little odd corner of a department were slung all sorts of oddments and remnants from a number of the grand upstairs departments. Anything in fact that was just worth saving rather than being thrown away.

The great Marshall Field toured the store itself regularly, accompanied by his entourage, but very seldom did he venture into the basement area. The stripling Selfridge's mother fed and housed him, so he laid out his scanty earnings wisely. So wisely, in fact, that he had twenty-four hours, secret information that next day Marshall Field was going to include a few minutes' visit to the basement.

This was the chance that the stripling had been planning for – for weeks he had been mugging up the tally of the principal oddments, but that was not all. As the junior boy it was his job to make a hot cup of coffee for all his half-dozen superiors. Next morning he did this with special relish and laced each strong cup with an aperient that he had tried on himself one Sunday after making very cautious enquiries from his mother's chemist.

The head of the little department was given thirty minutes notice of the grand inspection, but by that time he and all the others were scattered around trying to find a spare lavatory into which to lock themselves.

At the entrance it was explained to Marshall Field that a sudden attack had struck the staff, but up piped the diminutive Selfridge, who knew exactly what was here and what was there and how many yards there were in each roll. Marshall Field transferred him on the spot to be one of his personal runners (messenger boys, largely verbal, as telephones were either in their infancy or not invented).

And young Gordon proved to be the quickest and most accurate of all the half dozen, and so promotion came very quickly.

That is the end of the story of his "standing start". What happened afterwards was, of course, widely known at the time. Marshall Field made Selfridge his No. 2 and gave him a slice of stock in his company. But Selfridge overstepped himself (as he did again as an oldish man); he wanted the name of the store changed to Marshall Field and Selfridge. Marshall Field could not contain his anger. Selfridge was out and his stock purchased at a fair price. He always emphasized that.

Gordon Selfridge was then rich and in the prime of life. So he came to London and built his own store in Oxford Street. But he did not put a name on it outside — anywhere. It was then the grandest and greatest store in Oxford Street — so it did not need a name on its doors!

Ernest Simpson was a very early friend of mine from the 'twenties when we were both young men.

He had been in the Brigade of Guards during the latter half of the First World War and subsequently joined his old established family firm named, Simpson, Spence & Co. of Liverpool, who were and are what is known as forwarding agents.

In other words, they arranged for their many customers all that was necessary to move say, a load of motorcars from Coventry to New Orleans, USA. It is a very necessary and highly specialized business, particularly to the exporter of heavy and bulky manufactured goods and machinery such as that manufactured by Aveling-Barford Ltd.

His family firm had strong connections with the ports bordering the Caribbean Sea such as New Orleans, and in much later years, about 1950, he gave my then wife and myself most helpful introductions to some of his friends in that important shipping centre and port. This added greatly to our enjoyment of a short stay in that historic old city at the mouth of the Mississippi River.

But now I revert to earlier days when I met his wife who was to put him so much in the news, and who is now the Duchess of Windsor.

The Ernest Simpsons were then newly married and living at that time in the same block of flats, at Bryanston Court, as Grace and I, also newly married, but we didn't mix socially. I continued to see Ernest mainly at our mutual club, where, as a quiet unassuming chap, he was very popular.

I will now skip the years, the subsequent divorces and marriages which were headlines at the time, and stick to Ernest himself of whom I retain the happiest memories as a fine chap in every sense of the word, a good friend, and a most painstaking and successful host.

He fell ill – desperately ill – and it was clear to his relatives that there was no hope of recovery. His death was merely a question of time.

Eventually, it came to the point where his doctors decided that he could stand no more of the painful treatment so they sent him home to his flat in Eaton Square to die. Apparently, he asked his wife to invite a few of his long-standing pals together with their wives to a farewell party.

My then wife June and I went. There were only about twenty of us. Ernest could just about stand, he could not talk, but whispered, which was not easy to hear. I am telling this story to demonstrate his courage in the face of imminent death. He took my arm and I supported him from the room to his clothes closet. He fingered a new dinner jacket and motioned to me to do the same. I realized that it was made of some very expensive material, thin and soft to the touch.

I think the words he whispered were "Too late, Edward," and he was smiling broadly.

He never wore his new dinner jacket, because two days later he was dead.

Churchill and Beaverbrook were two men who had already crammed so much into their virile and exciting lives, so different in birth and achievement.

Physically, by 1940, they had done enough already. They had

each made their mark. And the deeper the mark the more numerous their supporters or detractors.

I have no personal knowledge of their pre-war personal relationship. I did not move in those circles. I heard only the chit-chat of
those who hoped they were impressing their neighbour at the
dinner table by exaggerating stories of which they did not know
the origin.

But as a lance-corporal of industry and as an ordinary citizen I
was convinced that I saw one truth clearly. Churchill used that
grand phrase "Their finest hour" about others. But the individuals
to whom this applied the most were himself and Beaverbrook.
I would also add President Roosevelt. I did not have the honour
of his acquaintance, and only once did I have a short conversation
with him. I did, however, become acquainted with Mrs. Eleanor
Roosevelt.

All three men had one experience in common. They had each
been criticized in previous years, in full measure. I did not say
"suffered" from criticism because I guess that they did not suffer.
Each hit back that bit harder. The Almighty had so arranged that
everything that had gone before had been tempering their iron
upon the anvil.

Now I must revert to the two Britishers about whom I am
entitled to write or speculate. I was not close to them, of course,
but no man can wear a poker-face mask twenty-four hours a day.

Some time before the beginning of his last fatal illness Lord
Beaverbrook telephoned me (please note the word telephone) and
said that he had been thinking back to that fight over the Grantham factories and those concerned with it. Something of importance or interest had happened together beyond the factories
themselves.

"I was interested at the time. There was a story. It might be
interesting, write it out and then we'll look at it together," said
the Lord, as he was called in Fleet Street.

I obeyed.

I had never been in his employ, but men of his calibre have
standards of their own. He was serving the British Empire: that is
how he saw it, and I was one of his part-time assistants; part-time
because I also had Aveling-Barford at Grantham to run as a
machine-gun carrier factory. I have said elsewhere that I had

over-reduced the staff at Grantham so that they could go to war. Having done this, I could not accept any whole-time London appointment in the wartime armaments hierarchy – much though I longed to do so.

I had an advantage over many others. I had had some acquaintance previously, and as a junior I had studied and watched both Churchill and Beaverbrook. I had the opportunity of watching them personally only from about 1937 onwards.

But it was very clear to me in 1940, that here were two men who realized very clearly and very simply that their finest hour had come. Both were fully middle-aged men, with Churchill a decade older.

Neither knew what diffidence meant. Immense self-confidence was at their core. Here was the greatest task that could be undertaken – the full equal to those that faced other great figures of history. So they helped themselves, and each other, to the Labours of Hercules and revelled in the task, because they were self-confident enough to be sure that there was no other Hercules available. I believe they were right.

My firm guess is that there was a sort of love-hate relationship between these two immensely powerful, self-willed, and egotistical personalities. Each was small in stature but, nevertheless, a veritable giant among men. In my view, there is nobody comparable alive today. I was not at all close to either of them in 1940 to 1942 but I did see a certain amount of them when they were "off parade" and as relaxed as was possible for them at that period of the war. And this is when the occasional unimportant but trusted onlooker and listener can see or sense "more of the game" than the important, official, high-ranking hierarchy. A fly on the wall can see a dictator with his pants down, as it were, even if it is only once a fortnight.

And so I make so bold as to give my personal guess, because as an occasional fly on the wall I watched, listened, and remembered all I bloody well could. Because my pin brain told me that each of these two men wanted to live in history a hundred years on. And they each wanted the same job – to be wartime Dictator of hard-pressed Britain. And each wanted the other as his No. 2. But each felt, and this is my sincere conviction, that he was better equipped than the other to keep Britain free from German domination.

Even the greatest of mortals in world history had feet of clay, and these two great mortals most certainly were no exception.

England in 1972 could certainly do with a reincarnation of one, or preferably both.

I used to meet Hugh Gaitskell quite a lot at Richard Stokes' little house in Westminster. Hugh and I both appreciated the luxury lovingly provided by Dick's two old servants from Ipswich.

With simple wholesome meals at fifteen minutes' notice at any irregular time, because these two old dears were concerned only with wholesome simple food for Dick, and up to three others, without more than a few minutes' warning.

When Hugh became Prime Minister (in moral fact though not in name) and Dick was Lord Privy Seal, the old dears still bullied them to "eat up to keep up their strength". It was fun and I think Gaitskell is still my favourite of the Bosses of England I have known.

Hugh Gaitskell paid me the great compliment twice of asking me to chair a government committee, first to "encourage the City of London to reform itself"; secondly, and about six months later, it was precisely the same, except that it was "The Law". Both these tentative offers are, of course, on cabinet record.

Some men among the Labour Party whom I have had the honour (and I use that word deliberately) to know, would have made admirable members of a dictatorship Cabinet if appointed when still at the height of their mental and physical powers.

Ernest Bevin, who was Ernie to all and sundry; was a truly great man. Great enough to change his mind and defy his critics if experience showed him that his first thoughts or views had changed. He would have become a great man in any age, with any background and in any sphere of activity, and even in the maelstrom of Party politics, his basic sincerity for the betterment of "all God's children" was clear.

Some two months before the dastardly assassination of President Kennedy, it had been arranged that Sir Alec Douglas-Home, then Prime Minister, would travel to Grantham to visit my factory and take luncheon with my management and myself before motoring back to Downing Street. This was a signal honour to a small but highly efficient exporting company.

Ten days before the appointed day, the world was shocked by the news of the assassination and it was quickly announced that the Prime Minister was flying to Washington for the funeral and would be out of England for over a week. Naturally my colleagues and I considered the Prime Minister's visit automatically cancelled, but our MP for Grantham, the great-hearted Joseph Godber, who had worked closely under Sir Alec in the Government, advised me not to cancel the arrangements as Sir Alec is a man of steel determination and a stickler for keeping his engagements.

Naturally I accepted Godber's advice and the short story is that the Prime Minister's special plane was diverted from Heathrow to Manchester due to weather conditions, but he still kept his date with Aveling-Barford.

The Chief Constable and other dignitaries sent me messages that the Prime Minister had brushed aside any suggestion of fatigue and he would visit Aveling-Barford on his road journey to London. He was bright and gay and cheerful. I thought then and I think still that here is a man in a million, and I could not discern any undue fatigue or strain on his face as we chatted over luncheon. We recalled a letter I had written to him, and here is an extract:

> You are by heritage a Scottish Laird of a very ancient lineage and you have thrown your coronet into the heather in the belief that this personal act serves Great Britain best. I cannot believe that you prefer swopping ruderies with Mr. Harold Wilson across the floor of the House to living in the home of your forefathers. You have already done more than your stint of public service. Every newspaper reader in Britain knows just as much about this as I do. They admire you tremendously for this act.

Adlai Stevenson was probably one of the most brilliant men I have ever had the opportunity of listening to. Our acquaintance-ship was slight and I met him perhaps half a dozen times, but I think that he should have held the world's most powerful role – President of the United States of America. My personal view is that he talked right above the heads of the average United States voters. They could not understand him, and he would not degrade himself by becoming a tub-thumper.

As a young man I received overnight hospitality from Henry Ford I. How this came about is an involved story so I will not go into details, but it was of course an honour to meet the great man in his simple smallish house.

After a dinner which thousands of his employees could have afforded, he asked me my ambitions: so I told him about road rollers. "How many a month?" he demanded.

"About forty or fifty," I replied.

He looked me over again and said sharply, "That's no business at all. That's chicken feed. Get into something at once with a worthwhile potential."

Using today's hindsight, I know that I had met a genius whose mind was entirely dedicated to quantity production. I am sure that the idea of spending five years building five power stations or five battleships would have appalled him!

No sensible person, weekly wage earner or not, can attempt to deny that Henry Ford I immensely enriched the world with his original Model T. He and he alone gave cheap motor transport to millions of ordinary folk such as the smaller farmers and traders via his network of distribution throughout the Americas. The model T Ford slashed costs almost everywhere, to universal benefit, with lower prices and much easier transport.

Even if a man of enterprise and vision were to retain one-hundredth part of the benefits for himself personally he becomes very rich. In almost every case he gives most of it away to benefit his fellow human beings.

It is indeed a splendid world asset that so many young men who started without any parental advantages have battled to the top in ways that better the ordinary daily life of a multitude of others. The personal wealth they accumulate is a small sliver compared to their value to their country and the vast amount of extra employment that they create.

Later there was William Morris at Cowley near Oxford. He started absolutely from scratch in England – a much smaller market – made a huge fortune, and then started to busy himself in giving almost all of it away. How much employment in all grades did he engender in Cowley, the site of his original tiny factory? I found him modest and charming, although by the time I knew him he was already a leading power in the motor industry. I lunched once at his home and was not surprised to find the same simple, modest establishment and way of home life as that of Henry Ford in America.

Then there was Herbert Austin whom I never met. His Austin 7 gave pleasure to millions of solid citizens.

These are three men from one industry only; a great industry that was not born until about a couple of generations after the agricultural implement makers (like my forbears) were firmly established.

It is private enterprise, particularly during the last few hundred years, that has brought great blessings in health and advancement in living standards for all of us who stand on two legs. Private enterprise is not perfect, but any society that deliberately tries to stifle it is putting the clock back to the living and health standards of the Plague of London or a few hundred years earlier.

Leylands, Britain's largest heavy lorry manufacturers, started in a small way and today their name is a household word. How immensely the development of this great business has benefited both the export trade and that part of the country where their main factory is situated. What a national tragedy it would be if today's group BLMC were to totter due to causes beyond their control. Some of us have great admiration for the success that Lord Stokes is already achieving in spite of the difficulties and problems being thrust in his path.

Britain needs much more private enterprise with chances to retain fair rewards coupled with huge reductions in bureaucracy and red tape. Let us all use our brains and experience to go forward faster rather than the bickering and niggling and the fomenting of discord which is so rife today.

In my opinion, Lord Carron ranked with the greatest of the Trade Union leaders. I first knew him as the local engineering trade union boss in Lincoln, when I was a director of Ruston & Hornsby about 1934 to 1937.

His life's work and endeavour was to improve the living standards and the status of the engineering chaps. But he equally saw both sides of the picture and dreaded the prospect of mass unemployment. His criticisms of management were accepted, discussed, and often acted upon. Equally, the majority of the weekly wage-earners recognized (somehow) that he was striving for the betterment of the engineering industry rather than only for nominal increases in wages.

It is indeed a pity, and maybe a tragedy, that men of his calibre seem to be replaced today by loud-mouthed trouble-makers who appear to gloat over creating the maximum discord and disruption to production.

Ten years before I met Carron, I knew Jimmy Thomas, the Right Honourable James Thomas, MP, a leading member of a Labour Cabinet. I repeat almost the same sentiments about him as a predecessor to Carron in the same field of trade union leadership.

Jimmy Thomas was sacked on the suggestion that he had betrayed to a certain individual a change in the rate of income tax a couple of days before the Budget speech. Naturally, a substantial amount of money could be made on the Stock Exchange in the event of such a leak from the Cabinet Room.

I never believed a word of it. But Jimmy was suspect in the Labour Party, apparently because he enjoyed the good things of life when they came his way through his own efforts and leadership. Like Ramsay MacDonald he wore "white tie and tails" (Fred Astaire's song) and a morning coat and top hat in the Royal Enclosure at Ascot. And why not?

I lunched with Jimmy Thomas at the Dorchester Hotel only a month or two before he died. We had a bottle of champagne, and it disappeared like lightning. He was one of the most amusing companions one could ever wish to know.

Simon Marks (later Lord Marks) was another man who would have been outstanding in any sphere: a small man with a big brain which he used to the full to the great advantage of his customers, his staff, and his shareholders. I do not know the size of Marks & Spencer before that genius of the Prudential, Lord May, backed Simon Marks and his colleagues heavily with additional capital, but it certainly proved to be a most happy and fruitful adventure to all concerned.

Simon had thought out his policy and methods most meticulously, together with a planned and regular rate of expansion. So far as I know, his colleagues and successors have seen no reason to depart from his original principles. Undoubtedly he must be awarded pride of place as the principal architect of what has grown steadily to such a vast organization.

Simon always said that there was no secret formula of success at Marks & Spencer, just clearcut policies known to all in the organization plus ability, hard work, and drive.

When in a relaxed mood he would enjoy answering questions about Marks & Spencer. And he just didn't know the meaning of the word swank. It is sad that Miriam, his consort and devoted wife, is now also dead.

At one time Kit Hoare was probably London's leading individual stockbroker. I knew him when his firm was named Cohen, Laming & Hoare – Hoare being the last addition. Today it is Hoare Govett, one of the greatest names in the City of London, but my memories are of Kit himself thirty-five years ago, and how he dominated his partners and almost everyone else he came into contact with.

He never wrote a letter if he could help it, and his secretary used a typewriter that was old fashioned even then and needed some form of blotter to make a duplicate or file copy, so that the chances were that the letter looked as if it had been soaking in a bath and was illegible.

Such trivialities didn't worry Kit. It was his brain, his personality and his quick assessment of fundamental facts that had got him right to the top of the tree in Threadneedle Street.

Now the wheel has turned so much that I believe Hoare Govett were the first stockbroking firm to invest in a computer.

I found it interesting when W. L. Dillingham told me about forty-five years ago that this chap Royce who was becoming famous because of Rolls-Royce was for a while a draughtsman's boy at Barford & Perkins.

W. L. Dillingham was the overworked and underpaid manager to my father and Mr. Perkins. Records in those times were rather sketchy compared with these grand days, when British industry is largely run by chaps who start as youths with qualifications like accounting and other national degrees. Dillingham had none except hit and miss with figures and a shrewd brain. His common-sense and loyalty to the business were not adequately appreciated by his employers, my father and Mr. Perkins; of that I am certain. He was just Dillingham, the manager and secretary, common clay compared with the owners and their families.

By the time I had been through my baptism of fire – the years in and out of hospital after March 1918 – I had come to appreciate the worth of this man, without whom or someone of equal quality, the two owners might have gone steadily downhill.

In his heyday (pre-war) Ambrose was such a feature of the Embassy Club that it was a signal honour if he paused for a second or so when leading his band with his violin to make a little motion with his bow or give the flicker of a smile to one of the dancers. Everybody tried to catch his eye but he was concentrating on his job. But just occasionally there was that flash of a grin or the momentary motion of his bow, and the girl in your arms was tickled pink. Yes, that's the way to describe it.

And now I come to about six years ago at the Sandy Lane Hotel, Barbados. For once I was holding myself upright to my six feet three inches as I hopped around the dancefloor, and both my partner (the owner of the Boutique and the sweetest and prettiest of the Island's residents) and I noticed that a small man – bald on top – was making signs of recognition.

I couldn't place him, but he also had a very attractive partner so I put the old memory box to work. It was, of course, Ambrose and later he introduced his partner, Miss Kathy Kirby. She told me the nicest things about him and how he had guided and helped her to stardom.

And I told her how much I had liked and admired him in the old Embassy days. It was, of course, well known that he was an inveterate gambler at the casino and that his style of music had fallen out of fashion. But we did quite a bit of reminiscing and I was glad to do it, because Bert Ambrose was the last chap to blow his own trumpet over past glories. After this reunion we used to meet occasionally. Delicious tuneful music tingled in his very blood and we were all made happier to listen to him.

Stanley Passmore was one of London's leading solicitors. He is now aged about eighty-five and his brain and joy in life and people are wonderful. He tells people, in front of me, "Until my partial retirement twenty years ago I had acted against Edward Barford four times. Three times he won because I hadn't got a case and the fourth was a draw."

His memory is still so keen and accurate that a couple of years ago we had several after-luncheon sessions at Buck's Club at which we fought our (legal) battles all over again. He is an outstanding example of the fact that it is not the date of your birth that matters. Some men are mentally old at sixty. Stanley is as bright as a cricket at eighty-five.

The Talent

If the good Lord has put into you at birth a reasonable brain, and if you yourself have bothered enough to develop and use that "talent" you are then a cut above your neighbours and those who started life on a par with you.

You must remind yourself often that your talent was born in you. It's no credit to you that you've got it, nor any reason for swank. Your job is to take the trouble and effort to make your talent grow to be increasingly useful both to yourself and to others, either locally or even nationally. It is doubtful if any man or woman has achieved great distinction in any field of human endeavour without firstly being born with a talent, and, secondly, without putting it to good use.

So if you have had enough savvy as a teenager to recognize this special gift in your brain, then bloody well go out and use it for all you are worth: in any walk of life that is becoming interesting to you.

Generally speaking, nobody really reaches the top and enjoys a fully satisfying life if he is in the wrong job. "Clock-watching" is a real tragedy. As soon as your family and domestic situation allows it, go firmly for what you know inside yourself is your real *métier*. And then you are set on the path – the right path for you.

I have always had a great love of Fleet Street and twice, once in 1926 and again in 1931, I planned to work there. But domestic and other financial responsibilities made it too difficult in 1926 – or so I thought then. I desperately needed a regular pay cheque to support me, my mother, and unmarried sister.

By 1948 my circumstances were rather different and I let it be known among the newspaper-owning families that I would pay £1 million for a slice of a national daily newspaper. A million then would be worth nearly three million today, but even so this sum would buy only a minor share; but I explained that any two leading firms of accountants could agree the size of the slice and I would accept their advice. But the two proprietors with whom I was then on Christian name terms said "no".

I still have regrets but overall I am glad, because though Fleet Street is today so lively and the main bulwark against Britain becoming a totalitarian state, many newspapers run at a financial loss. I put it very simply – our press are a great national safeguard to every man, woman, and child. Even the predecessors of the present Communist disrupters of orderly progress to a national higher standard of living realized this. These people find their pleasure working hard for dissension and strife instead of solid production in working hours.

Another ambition was to have a share in managing my country, which then again, twenty-three years ago, had an Empire. I did not think then and do not think today that Empire is a dirty word. I had agreed in general principle – when I was very small fry – with Lord Beaverbrook in his Empire Free Trade Campaign, although at that time I did not agree on all aspects of his proposals.

My talent at birth – I think I had a small one – enabled me to see a possible opportunity of becoming an important figure in Britain and, of course, the Empire. This was in 1946. I did not want to be a back-bench Member of Parliament with all the tediously slow advancement that this involves. Also, I loathe speechmaking and have always avoided it. Nor do I like kissing the babies of strangers, even though their parents have a vote. And I have always been an utter dud at remembering people's names, particularly when most needed. So a more unsuitable candidate for Parliament could not be imagined, although Tory Central Office were confident that the Grantham Division could be mine if I accepted. Well, I did not.

Am I sorry that I did not enter the political arena nearly twenty-five years ago? Certainly I should have striven not to remain a back-bencher for more than a year or two.

But already I had seen enough of the House of Commons to put me off it for life. I like it not. Nor do I have the sort of talent which makes a politician into a Cabinet minister. As I have shown in this book, my views are far too simple, clear, and forthright to suit any political party. Perhaps my own real talent has been to realize this!

Public Relations

Speaking cynically, a man is as good as he is judged to be by those millions of men and women whom nobody can ever fool. In fact, the truth can be very different.

A first-class public relations firm, given plenty of money to spend, can make the no. 3 man in any team of say a dozen into the no. 1, and will do the job so well that every ordinary average citizen in Britain is convinced that their client undoubtedly deserves to be no. 1.

But does anyone ever realize that the erstwhile no. 1 has been demoted by the public relations firm employed by no. 3? Our average citizen may be millions strong in numbers, but he doesn't know this trick.

And the trick is simple. No. 3 paid his public relations firm £100,000 a year—and so he became no. 1. The former no. 1 had arranged for only £30,000 a year to be allocated to public relations. So he got what he deserved and found himself demoted to no. 3. And both budgets were taken from the funds of the company, so the shareholders paid for the entire exercise, not no. 1 or no. 3.

It works equally well in every walk of life where it is important to be well regarded as a leader by our fellow men and women.

I first met one of the heads of a leading public relations firm around thirty-five years ago. In the Phoney War period of 1939 to 1940 I employed him (I'll call him X) to find a colour printer for a project which afterwards proved a huge success. Mr. Spalding, my publicity manager, with his usual ability and sixth sense, had managed to save a portion of the old Aveling & Porter "history" which was just about to be burnt as trash, before the great trek from Rochester to Grantham. I have always loved these evidences of the great Aveling heritage, and this was a chance to use old prints and photographs in an historical series of pictures. Spalding was equally enthusiastic. I supplied the ideas and he did all the work. The PRO's contribution in the final stages was negligible.

Just after the war I went to a cocktail party in X's large Mayfair conference rooms, and all round the walls were hung our historical series. He had Sir Billy Rootes (later Lord Rootes) and a dozen other magnates gathered round him and was addressing them in a loud voice. He told them that he had put this particular series around the conference rooms as it was one of the best jobs he had ever done. Then he caught sight of me joining the group and faltered. But only for a moment, and then he carried on bravely without lowering his voice. I admired him for that.

Shortly afterwards, he sought me out and apologized. I had no ill feelings, but he said that if we wanted his services again, he would do a job for practically nothing. Having got it clear that he meant this, I did use him again twice. For nothing.

The first occasion was in connection with an idea I had for driving the first of the post-war series of rollers at the opening ceremony over a bottle of champagne. The PR man thought the idea brilliant and got to work.

I knew Fleet Street pretty well by then; newspapers understandably avoid giving free publicity to any firm who can buy advertising space. The fact that only one in 20,000 people would be a potential purchaser of the hunks of machinery that we made did not alter this attitude.

Newspapers are like any other business. They have to sell enough of their product to make it pay. I hold the view strongly that much of the daily and weekly press is to be admired in that they do not print salacious filth which might well gain them much more circulation than they would lose.

Advertising revenue is of tremendous importance and this revenue depends very largely upon the paid circulation. I, therefore, feared that, even if we persuaded one national daily to print the photograph they would omit our name in the caption underneath.

All we really needed was our rampant horse design to show up prominently in the picture. As usual, my publicity manager understood perfectly and took over completely. My works director, E. R. Howlett, always co-operated splendidly in any of the stupidities which relaxed me so much and after a few shots of trial and error, i.e. painting and then photographing, they produced a fine "test" result and the horse on the front of the roller to be used was duly treated.

The caption I wrote went something like this:
"The world's greatest manufacturers of road rollers, Aveling-Barford Ltd. of Grantham, drive the first of a new series of rollers over a bottle of champagne at a christening ceremony presided over by Lord Brownlow, Lord-Lieutenant of Lincolnshire."

Directly after the opening ceremony I excused myself to my good friend Lord Brownlow, for Spalding was having the photographs developed at top speed and at the earliest possible moment a car was speeding to London.

The next morning was one of the happiest of my life. Every leading London daily carried the photograph and at least part of the caption, and most of them printed the lot. *The Times,* the *Daily Telegraph,* the *Daily Express,* and *Daily Mail* carried large photographs occupying a third or quarter of a page. I realized, of course, that we had been lucky to strike a dullish day so that there was no hot news competition. It was terrific, and the provincial and Scottish dailies followed suit, in an equally large way.

The public relations firm totted it all up and said we have been given £250,000 worth of free publicity.

In my view, it was not worth more than £5,000 to £10,000 to us. But there are often factors to be considered. Every public relations man or woman knows that a reference in the newspaper proper is ten times as valuable as a paid advertisement. And youths grow into men, and some may enter the civil engineering world. All sorts of men and women, who may never previously have heard our name, sit on councils, and maybe are vaguely aware that a road roller or two gets purchased from time to time because they have to pass the necessary minute at a meeting.

It can do nothing but good for a small firm to be well known — unless of course the reason for the free publicity falls into that other category, such as "Aveling-Barford of Grantham regrets to announce that all salary and wage payments are stopped because the Chairman has used his pass key and absconded to South America with all the available cash".

The second occasion I took advantage of X's offer was when my sales manager showed me a photograph taken about a fortnight previously of a number of our rollers loaded up as a trainload for shipment to Burma. He was in the process of sending it to our trade periodicals. Spalding and I immediately had a hurried conference. We could not take a more suitable photograph because the consignment had left a fortnight before. Spalding, however, doctored up the horse on the leading roller and enlarged the photograph so that the horse finally looked about the size of the whole of the first roller. We did not think anyone would notice anything odd about this, and they did not.

The papers had been mentioning the huge number of Indians who were at that time dying of starvation and that the Government of Burma were quickly repairing roads and railways to rush as much rice as they could to India. Everyone at Grantham had read this, because there had been several press articles and references to this famine during the previous fortnight. But nobody had realized what an opportunity this gave us for publicity.

Off I sent the photograph to London with a caption something like this: "The world's largest makers of road rollers, Aveling-Barford Ltd. hurry off a trainload to Burma for repairing roads that will bring rice to the starving millions of India."

It was the greatest sell-out, exactly like the first. Our name was left in throughout and the horse showed up beautifully.

The public relations firm was delighted. It enhanced their reputation, and presumably they got a good price for the photographs – but they got nothing from me.

Advertising rates had risen a good deal between 1940 and 1947 so this time the calculation of free publicity was £300,000. X considered he had repaid his debt to me, and I agreed.

Actually the rollers in question had been on order before the famine had become so acute. I gave special priority for delivery in the hope of playing some small part in alleviating human suffering if transport of the rice could be expedited.

But the *bonne bouche* was that I learned months afterwards the Crown Agents had shipped them on about the slowest steamer afloat. This was her last voyage before being sold for scrap. The Crown Agent himself, Sir James Carmichael, who had seen the newspapers, supplied me with this final titbit and stood me a couple of drinks at his club.

Sir James, a great Proconsul, was the last man to hold the proud title, Crown Agent to the Colonies. In those days, England ran a quarter of the globe and every Briton or foreigner knew it.

It is true that some foreigners or foreign officials did not always quite understand what a British passport meant and arrested a drunken able seaman in a dive of a foreign port without notifying both the British Consul and the captain of the ship from which this limey hailed.

I am confident that fifty years from now, historians will agree generally that those were the days when, generally speaking, right was right and wrong was wrong.

The Crown Agents

I remember being told in several Crown colonies, as they were then, including Malaya, that Aveling steam rollers were the first pieces of machinery to be imported and owned by the public works department. Sir James Carmichael was courteous enough to have the old records turned up, and they confirmed that this was true.

I must repeat that until a few decades back all public services and buildings came under the Director of Public Works, even down to hospital equipment, and if a planter or estate owner wanted some technical or mechanical advice he went to them as the people most qualified and most willing to be friendly and helpful on any matter that benefited the Colony. Sometimes their problems were referred to the Crown agent's building opposite the Houses of Parliament in London; also upon a non-paying basis.

And what did the Crown agents charge the colonies for their services, quite apart from those that they gave freely? Most of us have had experience of the post-war charges of government agencies for doing practically nothing. What did the Crown agents charge in the days when England had an Empire? Is fifteen per cent or twenty per cent your guess? Well, two per cent would be nearer the mark, but in those days the few bureaucrats and their Cabinet ministers bothered about each thousand pounds. Today's huge army of bureaucracy throws millions about like pennies.

People like my great-grandfather and grandfather, and many others who built up much larger enterprises, were adventurers. Most of the old family general engineering businesses were founded by men who were brought up and trained to serve the greatest industries in the world—the land and food. Perhaps they were small squires, perhaps tenant farmers, perhaps only farm workers. But they left the work they had been steeped in since birth, as had their forbears before them, and risked any savings they had accumulated, for the great adventure of making machinery for foreign parts (as they were then called).

The dandy chaps who now rule us in our private and business lives through their hordes of officials write charmingly phrased, general, and genteel exhortations to British industry to increase export trade (now better phrased, so probably they are written by a public relations firm).

The cost of all this official machinery to help and advise exporters is "something terrible". Since it is all borne out of taxes, it puts up the price of Britain's exports. But lots of lads and lassies, who know nothing whatever about the usual processes of a firm which has been exporting for 100 years and have only a nodding acquaintance, if that, with the foreign country they are writing about, have a lovely easy life in some of the most expensive offices in London.

But now a quarter of the world is no longer anxious and willing to buy from us. At the present time it is just a hard fight between Britain and her competitors. No unfriendliness, but no sentiment or thoughts to the distant past, either. And the devil take the hindmost. However much any politician may blab or bluster in Parliament or press, the simple fact is that any Party in power can control only just these islands and a few miles of sea surrounding them. When you listen to or read some of the debates you may think it is just as well. England must export or die.

A Tribute to My Most Constant Companion

For thirty-nine years every night of every day of every year, it has slept under the same roof, been in the same ship or plane, car or under the same bed while I was snoring topside – or more pleasantly engaged. For thirty-nine years it has been my everyday companion from rags to riches, with some sharp and unpleasant reverses in the meanwhile. I am referring to my business case.

When I first acquired it I was in very serious debt and going deeper every month. Of course I couldn't afford a car – even by the day – and though taxi drivers (the salt of the earth, London

Cockneys) let you get out of the cab before paying, they can well turn nasty if you try to walk away saying in a loud aristocratic manner "put it down to me".

In those days some chaps had major-domos or butlers awaiting their arrival at their stately town house and these chaps descended with dignity to pay off the lowly taxi, while a footman bowingly ushered the gilded youth within. But that was not for me. I have never been envious but I thought that a superior-looking small case might look well, if I ever succeeded in reaching the presence of those city magnates and joint general managers of banks from whom I had youthful hopes of borrowing enough dough to set myself up in business of my own.

My little brochure – my case was four years old by then – so cleverly compiled by the great Sir Charles Palmour of Whinney, Smith, and Whinney, contained all my dreams, but could not be crushed into my pockets, together with all my other more detailed memoranda and old balance sheets signed by Price Waterhouse and Company. I needed something to carry all the typed and written matter that I had compiled during so many sleepless nights.

Young or youngish men are fortunately full of optimism, and I also wanted a case that would not cause raised eyebrows from the doormen of such hotels as Claridge's, then exclusively exclusive and frequently used by high and mighty Kings of Finance – intermingled with foreign royalty. In those days one just could not be seen walking into a St. James's Street club carrying anything that could possibly be thought to contain anything that might be connected with trade or commerce or finance. It was all condemned together as trade, and the whole thing was just "not done".

And so I went to Mr. Lansdowne. He did not sell ready-made luggage or anything as common as that, but he made beautiful leather luggage to order – to measure – to suit the client. His clientele naturally were mainly of aristocratic birth so the cases were suitably emblazoned with coronets or coats of arms with the owner's name and rank carefully, but not too prominently, embellished upon them. After all, rank was rank still in those days and rough chaps like station porters might as well know the honour conferred upon them when carrying stately baggage.

I conferred with Mr. Lansdowne and with the aid of a tape measure and some foolscap sheets I had brought with me, I told him the size of case I wanted, fifteen inches long, nine inches wide, and two inches deep – just big enough to take foolscap sheets. I wanted it made of pigskin, with best quality shiny locks. Everything of the best throughout.

This was a great extravagance. Mr. Lansdowne had never made a case like it. Business cases were clumsy and bulky things in those days. He thought that this might set a new trend, particularly if it ever got as far as being seen by the influential. He was, and is, a charming chap but I think he realized that I could well do with a new suit and a new pair of shoes. He said he would consult the foreman of his little factory outside London and let me have an estimate in a few days.

He did and I confirmed my order. The price? That will remain secret until the end of this ode and tribute to my beloved friend.

My case was certainly the first of its slim shape. No shop, Bond Street, Jermyn Street, or otherwise then had anything to sell so smart and shapely. I never saw another and many people asked me where I had it made. Within two years Lansdownes were doing quite a large exclusive trade making them of course individually by hand. Today, fashion has changed and much more elegant soft leather business wallets are on sale everywhere.

When my case was seven years old, my finances had emerged from the red at long last and I had become a director of that fine company whose roots in British engineering were nearly as old as those of my own forbears, I was able to give a number of cases away to friends I had then acquired, such as prominent business and professional chaps and particularly to the then chairman and the two managing directors of Ruston & Hornsby.

My business case has always carried some notes on my personal finances for me to browse over and ensure that I do not get "into the red" again. Its contents have recalled to me that the pound sterling of only thirty years ago is now a mere miserable four bob. My case and I say that the pound sterling is no friend of ours.

On business trips abroad and on holidays, my case has contained travellers' cheques or instructions from London banks to the appropriate affiliated banks in many parts of the world, but never more than perhaps £10 in actual cash in any currency. Even so, its contents have almost invariably been invaluable to me and virtually irreplaceable.

I use the word virtually with deliberation. Most of its contents have been either in my own handwriting or typed by my confidential secretary. If I were to go into purdah for six months with a cold towel round my head daily for seven hours, six days a week, I could replace the written or typed portions. Bank authorities or summarized balance sheets can be replaced. That's simple enough.

From its very early youth, I had developed a fixed routine of locking both locks whenever I put any paper in or took it out; usually about fifty times a day. More than a million turns of the lock in thirty-nine years.

My case and its original locks have earned retirement although there is nothing to suggest that they could not give equally good service for many more years.

Its retirement is purely sentimental. And the cost of this made-to-measure case in pigskin — £4 4s. od.!

But then that was thirty-nine years ago. Today's price is thirty guineas.

Control by Bureaucracy

Unfortunately talent can be stifled by bureaucracy, and here in Britain we know all about that particular disease.

About twelve years ago we had frequent telephone trouble at my country home in Hertfordshire, and the telephone engineer was a constant visitor, although a considerable period usually elapsed between our reporting the 'phone out of order and his arrival. He was an intelligent, youngish chap and he explained his routine to me. He said he could easily do on his own the work for which four men, together with vans, were now employed, if he were allowed to plan out his daily visits for himself, and if breakdowns in service were reported to him direct. On his suggesting this and asking for a twenty per cent rise in salary, his proposal had been curtly refused. So he was taking a job in private electrical industry.

Are there thousands of similar cases of waste in all the services monopolized by the Post Office? Probably there are tens of thousands, but who cares? Just shove up the charges once again, and if that's not enough, yet again after that. After all, this is a monopoly.

Although I have been a telephone subscriber for well over forty years and have never failed to pay a bill, I receive almost regularly curt printed notices threatening to cut off my telephone because I have not paid the bill. More often than not I have not even received the bill in question. Last time the bill arrived two days after the threatening notice!

An ordinary private enterprise shopkeeper would apologize if his bookkeeper meted out such treatment in genuine error. But do our little dictators, the state monopoly? They are our masters, and they know it. We are their cringing underlings, and we know it, too, for a telephone is today a necessity.

When I bought my home in the country from the Co-operative Society, who had planned several years previously to use it as a convalescent home, the property included four wooden cottages in a block that should certainly have been condemned for human habitation many years before.

I must emphasize that I did not want or need these miserable cottages in their existing state; nor did I need them in a repaired state, nor did I need four new cottages. I had done up other cottages thoroughly and had enough for my farm employees. However, the cottages were still inhabited and the tenants paid me a rent of two shillings a week per cottage. This was obviously a major attraction, since by law I could only increase the rent by a third, which would add another eightpence a week.

I suggested that the local authorities should inspect the cottages afresh and, in the event of their agreeing with me that they were unfit for human habitation, build four council houses to replace them. For these I would willingly donate the land, provided that the occupants of the four wooden cottages were given first refusal of the new houses. This was merely a friendly neighbourly gesture to the existing tenants who were not in my employ nor had they anything to do with me.

The reply came a couple of months later when I was served with an "official" order instructing me to carry out major rebuilding works in order to make the cottages habitable. I was ordered to spend about £8,000 on the buildings, and they weren't worth more than £400 or so for scrap! They had been shoved up carelessly in the First World War, obviously just to last a few years at most. Each had two tiny rooms on the ground floor and two above

There was no bathroom, nor room for one, no lighting, heating, or water, and the primitive lavatory to serve all four cottages was fifty feet at the back. It was an absurd suggestion that I try to rebuild the cottages, but it was also an order and the authorities persisted with increasing threats, emphasizing their powers of dictatorship.

I employed two architects, and they both said the same thing — namely, that the cottages were a complete write-off and that it would cost more to put them in order than to build four new ones. Still the authorities persisted, saying that they were only exercising powers invested in them by law.

Then I had a brainwave. Only a year or two previously my friend, Sir Andrew Clark, QC, had toppled the Minister of Agriculture off his throne over the Crichel Down affair. I knew the Minister, a very nice and able chap, but under our present system how can a minister of the Crown know the iniquities that may be perpetrated in his name?

I didn't look up the law in the matter, but simply wrote to the authorities saying that if they really insisted on my rebuilding the four cottages then they would have to take me to court over it. In that case I told them I intended asking my solicitors to retain Sir Andrew Clark, QC to appear for me. This was a big name and a big personality to bring into a small country court, and my suggestion had the effect I had anticipated.

My letter was obviously passed right up the line to senior officials, and the whole thing was suddenly dropped. All that time wasted by officialdom (and we pay their ever-increasing costs). And all my time and money, too, to protect my rights as a citizen!

The cottages were officially condemned and the tenants found other accommodation. One at least, who had his grown-up son living with him — they were both earning good money in the building trade — was very sorry to go and complained bitterly that his rent was being increased about fifteen times.

The cottages are still there and for many years we had good use for them; hundreds of chickens apparently found them a happy home.

When I first bought my home the electricity was often well below the proper voltage, so that the lights flickered and dimmed, as did the electric fires. The television was sometimes on and sometimes off. It was explained to me that our particular cable was overloaded, particularly when neighbouring farmers were using their electric milking machines for their cows. The authority, therefore, would put in a larger cable, but since I was to be the principal beneficiary I must contribute substantially to the cost.

With some reluctance I agreed to these terms and all went well for about three years. Then the same thing began to happen again. A number of additional consumers had been hooked on the new cable, which had now become as overloaded as the first one. Naturally I received neither redress nor the return of my money, because that's how the machine works. It is just a waste of time for a private citizen to try to fight the machine single-handed.

It is the duty of government so to organize its monopolies as to make it almost impossible for private citizens to be bullied or browbeaten by one or another government department.

One Friday evening I found waiting for me at home four officials who had driven up in a large Humber car. They explained that they were from the Electricity Board and that they had called several times previously but had not found me at home.

This had already happened with other government departments and agencies, so I was not surprised at this waste of time and public money. There is no point in using the telephone to make an appointment when you can take a nice country drive in a large car, and if the chap is not at home you can adjourn to a good restaurant in the vicinity and have a slap-up meal at the taxpayers' expense. Why use the telephone and spoil an outing?

Anyway, they explained to me that they were going to put up an electricity pylon on my land, just near my gardener's cottage, and there was nothing I could do about it. Then they produced a long official document which would take some time to read through and asked me to sign it there and then. I refused and told them to leave the document with me. My solicitors perused it subsequently but told me there was really nothing I could do about it, so I signed it and sent it back. And, in due course, up went the pylon.

The same thing happened with about six pylons about 750 yards away from my front door. If they had been put fifty yards further away they would have been on the other side of a country road and screened by two hedges. There are no cottages or houses that side, so nobody would have been affected and it was almost all my farmland, anyway. But, no, they had planned it that way on a map, and they had powers to use any part of my land they chose.

They were the dictators. I was merely the landowner whose simple and reasonable wishes could be completely disregarded.

There are two personal examples, and the reader has probably experienced as much or more. Big things, little things: the huge army of officialdom uses the taxpayers' money to beat him to his knees.

One class of thieving by government became so prevalent, that it even stopped being news enough to appear in the press. I refer to the business of compulsory purchase. Old ladies find that the home they have lived in all their lives is suddenly purchased from them compulsorily, at a figure fixed by officialdom, which thinks itself clever to give the poor old dears much less than the property's current value.

The official excuse, of course, is that the site is required for some improvement in the public interest. The old ladies are duly dispossessed and if they are lucky they die of a broken heart, but nothing happens to the site. The officials have changed their minds and no longer require it. Eventually, it is sold to someone else for ten or fifteen times as much as they gave to the old ladies. The reader ought to be wondering, as I am, why they don't let the old ladies or their heirs buy the house back for the figure at which they were forced to sell it and give them fair compensation for having been turned out. But that would be too sensible and humane for officialdom.

The next time one of our legislators suggests in my presence that all is well in this world of bureaucracy and small-time dictators, I shall feel like spitting in his face.

To the ordinary citizen, government departments are faceless. You don't even know what individual you are dealing with. An underling may be ordering you about without authority from above, or he may have obtained such authority by showing bias against your case.

But the ordinary citizen owns these departments and pays for them in crushing taxation. Let them be made to serve us, not bully us. Let some government, any government, embark upon the task of giving freedom within the law to the individual. Let them set

WHAT HAPPENED TO THE COW THAT GOT IN THE WAY OF A **BARFORD & PERKINS** ROLLER

In about 1923 I was personally engaged on most of the catalogues for Barford & Perkins Ltd. I wrote the script, from information given to me by the design and drawing departments, selected the illustrations and supervised the printing. I found it most interesting and it also helped me to learn something of the engineering side of which I was totally ignorant.

One of the things I did was to commission Heath Robinson, then probably the leading cartoonist in England, to carry out some work for us. One of his cartoons is shown here. It was the cover of a small booklet which was forwarded to our overseas agents for them to pass on to the customers. This particular cartoon was widely distributed in India before somebody in the office of our agents realised that, because the cow is a sacred animal in India, the cartoon could cause offence. And it did! Every effort was made to get the booklets back to our agent's office in Calcutta where they could be burned on their own funeral pyre (as it were).

Will my readers use their brains and tell me whether there is any parallel (or a ghost of one) here with Party manifestos prior to general elections? Do they get quietly burnt after the ballot boxes have had their say?

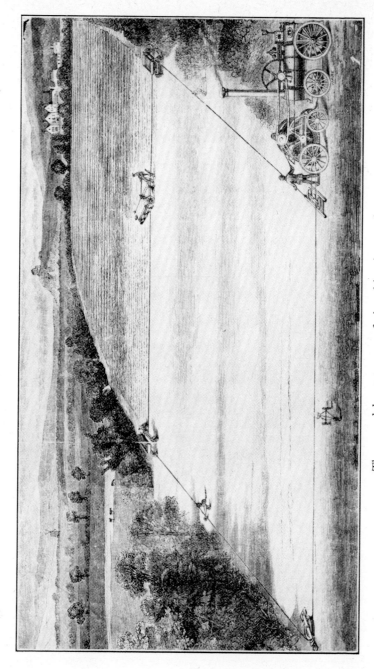

The roundabout system of ploughing invented about 1865 by William Barford.

The first steam roller, in London's Hyde Park
(reproduced from the *Illustrated London News*, 15th
December 1866)

The first steam roller in America, working in New
York's Central Park in 1869. The original illustration
appeared in the same year in the publication, *Engineering*.

The first steam roller in the streets of Liverpool (*Illustrated London News*, 12th October 1867).

Britain free – and then they need never fear the result of any subsequent General Election.

Some Needed Reforms

I see the square mile of the City of London from the outside, but even so I have had thirty years' experience of looking through the windows, and I have many friends, both business and social, who work inside.

Nobody doubts that fully eighty per cent of the chaps who work there are thoroughly honest. But it has seemed to me for many years that their methods and machinery need modernizing thoroughly to protect small investors, who today may number millions, whose savings are the result of painstaking thrift over many years.

They are virtually powerless (as I have shown earlier in this book in my own personal experience) and the Big Wigs of the City of London have done far too little in a solid and practical sense, though they are careful to protect their own profits and gains. Naturally, one's personal observations show that the Stock Exchange Committee have slowly become more and more vigilant over the last few decades, but I assume that this is a voluntary body of leading and able men whose natural instincts are that their particular area of the City of London should "keep its nose clean".

On balance, it is perhaps a disadvantage that nepotism in all its forms has been so firmly rooted in the City of London for so many generations. It is therefore splendid for the national interest that in 1972 there are so many bright chaps of humble origin who have broken right through the upper crust of lineage and beaten – honestly – the system of nepotism.

Nepotism is a natural part of everyday life, but the City of London appears to the interested onlooker to have more than its share of it.

Collectively, small investors are probably the most valuable national asset in Britain today – solid, respectable, upright citizens who have retained both the wish and the power to think for themselves and the sense of independence that goes with it. They are not believers in support by the State "from cradle to grave". They would prefer lower direct and indirect taxation resulting from

huge slashing (not gentle pruning) of the vast army of bureaucracy, so that they can save more and invest those savings in a
manner which they hope will at least keep abreast of riproaring
inflation, and perhaps even beat it.

These folk comprise the backbone of Britain and are the steady-
ing influence in the electorate as a whole. Their existence as a huge
body of small potential investors has been increasingly recognized
by the City of London over the past ten or fifteen years, and much
money has been spent by the City, particularly in newspaper
advertisements, to attract their money which averages, I think, a
few hundred pounds apiece.

These men and women understand their own job and play their
part well in local and family life, but when it comes to investment
they have been, and are, newcomers so that a proportion of them
fall victims to downright swindling and robbery, much of which
is still perfectly legal today.

I am not so ignorant as not to be aware that a good deal has
already been done in this field, but it is palpably obvious that it has
been much too little and often much too late.

The swindlings of the last ten or fifteen years have only been
mentioned in newspapers or on radio or television if they have
been sufficiently large and barefaced to be "news" to millions, as
opposed to a few hundred or thousand victims. And the thieves
are not even stripped of the money they have stolen. A spell in a
healthy prison and then the swindlers come bouncing out again,
full of energy to enjoy the money they have virtually stolen from
so many small savers.

In spite of some safeguards, introduced mainly during the last
twenty years, it is clear that crime still pays very handsomely
indeed, particularly if the criminals are prepared to risk a few years
working say in a prison library and under such mild restraint as is
now considered adequate by the senior officials who are required
to carry out in daily detail the woolly-minded general principles
emanating from the House of Commons.

In my view, the small investor should invest his money in Unit
Trusts, all of which emphasize that share prices can go down as
well as up. The professional managers of these know the dishonest tricks of the sharpsters, so investors have no reason for
worry even if world or other events push stock prices down,

probably very temporarily, because the spur of competition in private enterprise is very sharp and real and keeps management right on its toes.

For larger investors, investment trusts are better.

But what have successive chancellors of the exchequer done to catch and punish sharply the twister or the downright swindler? Often a big name on a board of directors influences investment. If this chap smells or suspects bad news, he can resign overnight and sever all connections with the company. This is both cowardly and dishonest, but legal.

Directors fight any inquisitive shareholders with the shareholders' own money, so it is immaterial what the directors spend to protect their personal position and reputation. Again, this is legal. Once the general public has bought the shares, they are often nearly defenceless and if a few shareholders feel they have cause for complaint or even information they must collect a fighting fund from their own pockets—and no tax relief either.

This disgraceful situation could be improved vastly and easily though complete protection may be impossible (as some of my friends allege).

Of course, the scene of the City of London has changed greatly over the last thirty or forty years, during which we have seen the vast growth of the great insurance corporation, which preceded the investment trusts, and unit trusts.

It is much to the credit of the management of these huge institutions that they have demonstrated clearly and publicly their full appreciation of the responsibilities they carry as custodians of enormous total sums of money belonging to hundreds of thousands of small investors.

I repeat that the committee and management of the Stock Exchange have certainly been moving in the right direction. But who comes out and takes the risk of open castigation by name? Our laws of libel are a relic of past ages and often protect the wrongdoer. "The greater the truth, the greater the libel."

Within the space available in their columns, City editors try to protect the public. I take off my hat to them.

Reforms are also long overdue in the fields of leasehold law and accountancy. The laws relating to leasehold property should have been amended many years ago, and it is surprising that the subject has still not been tackled.

Over the last 300 to 500 years there has been colossal inflation, especially during the last 100 years. What once cost threepence or sixpence, now costs £1 sterling. Properties which 300 years ago were open fields around the small town that was then London are now residential areas in Knightsbridge, Chelsea, Kensington, and St. John's Wood. And the value of the original fields has multiplied scores of times over.

Vast areas of land then particularly near large towns, were leased for ninety-nine years to people who erected buildings upon them; houses, shops and the like, entirely at their own expense, paying a ground rent to the landlord. Under the terms of the leases, the land, together with the buildings erected on it, reverted to the landlords when the leases expired. Nobody wants laws to be passed which have the effect of breaking legal contracts between the original landlords and the present tenants, but this is a major issue. The passage of time, and other factors, have made reform necessary.

In view of rises in values, sometimes from £500 to £10,000 or more in one lifetime, it should be possible to have the position carefully reviewed by a committee appointed by the government, with very simple terms of reference. All the committee would be required to do, in fact, is suggest to Parliament a simple formula to give a price at which the tenant can buy the property from the landlord.

I have never heard of representations being made to the accountancy profession by any government. The existing system of presenting audited accounts probably worked very well forty or fifty years ago, but the whole thing could be done, and should be done, in a much easier and simpler way. I feel that the government should encourage the profession to submit proposals for simplifying the job, proposals which could be vetted by the Federation of British Industries and the Institute of Directors on the one hand, and by the trade unions and their representatives on the other.

It should be possible for anyone who can read and write to see, simply and clearly, what profit on each pound of capital any company is making. Also what proportion of this is to be distributed to the risk-taking shareholders and how much is being ploughed back for modernization, expansion, and improving the prospects of higher wages for all in future years.

Then the general public become more knowledgeable and better informed. Much progress has already been made but much more mumbo-jumbo has been retained quite unnecessarily – presumably for the self-glorification of the accountancy profession.

At present, annual reports are mainly stated in antiquated accountancy jargon which leaves many men and almost all women entirely at sea. What is wrong with simple use of the English language? Again, we have the City editors to thank for putting simple facts in simple language. Many companies are now helping by buying newspaper space to give salient figures only from their annual general meetings. Why should not the accountancy profession modernize itself and do the same? Perhaps they would prefer to go backwards and write their jargon in Latin like doctors' prescriptions?

The general public are all voters now at the age of eighteen. Give them the chance to see how good management, working under and often side by side with bosses with ideas can produce national wealth and a higher standard of living all round.

Brains and initiative are prized very highly in almost every country in the world except here in Britain. Here, many Communist shop stewards regard it as a crime that the engine driver who has the safety of a trainload of men, women, and children in his hands, should be paid more highly than a man with a routine job on the railways. It is the same with management. We openly and deliberately spend the taxpayers' money, which is money raised annually by taxes from all of us, on education, and then we deprive Britain of this national asset by crippling tax and surtax.

For instance, many very highly trained doctors and surgeons emigrate because of taxation so our National Health Service imports replacements from abroad often with less training, experience, and skill! Could anything be more stupid?

If democracy in 1972 has come to mean that loudmouthed tub-thumpers and shady politicians, both local and national, gain control at the poll boxes, then the sooner we invite the late Mr. Moses back from limbo, and put him on his Mount, the better both for us and for succeeding generations.

Poem by Evoe

I now reprint a poem of which I am very fond. This is how it came to be written.

The late E. V. Knox was a leading contributor to the magazine, *Punch*, for many years and I was among the multitude of his admirers. I had not then met him. Finally I did so through the kind offices of his nephew, Simon Elwes, the portrait painter, who is a very old friend of mine.

E. V. said that as a boy he had been fascinated by the rural district steam roller which was often working near his home and he always wanted to drive it. He still felt upset at the sight of a road roller driven by a petrol or diesel engine. He was obviously so knowledgeable about the methods of road repair with tarmacadam as practised in his youth that I suggested he should write a poem for *Punch* expressing his lament. "The Death of a Dream" was the result.

Those who are old enough to remember the old tarmacadam days will also know how accurate this poem is. The piece of road to be repaired was barred off and there were red flags at either end; the black tar was heated and sprayed out of barrels on to the roadstone or flint.

THE DEATH OF A DREAM

("Steam-roller. 1866. A heavy locomotive engine with wide wheels used for crushing road-metal and levelling roads, b.fig. (colloq.) A crushing power or force, 1902." – O.E.D.)

> It was never my dream to drive a train
> Nor to act as a world controller,
> I had set my soil on the nobler goal
> Of a Rural District roller:
> For its hey to be up betimes, my lad,
> And list to the hedge bird's carol
> And a crank to wind and a road to grind
> And the tar running out of the barrel.

It's hey to be up with the lark, my lad,
And one good fellow-toiler
And a flag to guard, and a way well barred
And a head of steam in the boiler;
For who would care to fly through the air
Or to cleave the waves asunder
When to and fro he could loudly go
To the sound of his own sweet thunder?

The books I left to the cleverer boys
And the aim at wealth or station,
For a rolling life has its own sweet joys
And a time for contemplation;
I longed to be prince of a world of flints
And lord of a pitch-black runnel
And a stoked-up fire and a word from squire
And the sparks flying out of my funnel.

But today I have seen a terrible sight
In the gloom of a mist-dark dawning
That ground the stones with the same old groans
And the same old bed-top awning,
And the crest of Kent in the forefront went,
But it could not be forgiven –
It had spoilt the fame of an ancient name
FOR THE THING WAS PETROL-DRIVEN.

Solemn and strong it rolled along
With a grave and ponderous motion,
And little it cared as it slowly fared
It had lost a heart's devotion;
For many a changing chance I've seen
And time is a great consoler,
But I cannot be friends with gasoline
In a Rural District Roller.

EVOE

(Reproduced by permission of the Proprietors of *Punch*)

The First World War

One thing became very clear to me soon after I reached the fighting line about the middle of 1916.

Our side, particularly those who had already been in the war for a year or more, were just sick and tired of the whole thing. I cannot describe the muck, the filth, the squalor, the human degradation of that time in printable language. Where there had been heavy fighting previously, almost every shellburst threw up corpses, both British and German, and the stench was indescribable. There is a limit to bravery, as men had discovered hundreds of years before when submitted to daily torture on the rack until they confessed to something entirely untrue. When a man is worn out, physically and mentally, his courage, or a great deal of it, oozes away too.

Men who had reached this stage went over the top or cut wires in No Man's Land like automatons, because an officer or an NCO issued the command, because it was always being drilled into them that they would be shot for cowardice if they didn't. As far as I know, we were all frightened, but we were still more frightened of showing it or betraying it to others.

Even then it was clear that all this held good for the other side as well, and to those younger men who think there is anything glorious in war, I recommend that fine book by Erich Maria Remarque, *All Quiet on the Western Front*. It was clear that one of the things our higher command was most concerned about was that any small outbreak of fraternization between even a few soldiers on either side would quickly spread like wildfire and war in that area would come to a stop. If that had happened and the officers, true to their code, had tried to shoot the men's ring-leaders, then the men would have overpowered their own officers.

The first time I shot a German face to face my feelings were typical of anyone's. In an unspoken sort of way I had absorbed those feelings from others.

I was observing the effects of our own shell fire from as forward a position as I could reach, and was using a trench which I thought was deserted by both sides. But in negotiating a buttress my head collided with another head coming the other way. The trenches were almost always shallow so that you had to walk along bent double. I was about to pump up a laughing apology when I suddenly realized the man was a German. My revolver was in its holster with the flap undone and somehow or other I managed to get it out before he got his. I shot him twice, in the stomach, at about three feet away. My first shot must have hit him as he squeezed the trigger because his hand shot up and the bullet went into the air. He was obviously dying fast, but I just didn't have the heart to finish him off in cold blood with a bullet through the temple. I had to leave him. I went about 200 yards away and continued my job of observing our shell fire.

Half an hour later I went back and was much relieved to find that he was dead. He was a German major. I took off his identification tabs, then looked again. He had a fine automatic pistol which he should have been able to draw and fire far quicker than I could with my heavy Colt revolver. I took the pistol and all its ammunition, and also a fine pair of binoculars. I still have the binoculars and I use them at race meetings and at Wimbledon. The pistol was wrested from me some years ago by the Hertfordshire police.

The Germans weren't our only enemy in that war and nor was the mud, the filth. There was also the casual attitude of the British War Office towards the ordinary soldier. Our uniforms didn't fit – anything would do so long as it didn't come within inches of your right size. The food we had would be condemned today as unfit for animals. It was either under-cooked or over-cooked. Sometimes all you got was a great lump of fat. The bread was always stale, and often filthy-dirty. The margarine was rancid and smelt appalling. At mealtimes the orderly officer of that day came round asking, "Any complaints?" Heaven help the chap who stood up and said "yes".

It was all a shabby way to treat those who had heeded Kitchener's appeal "Your King and Country Need You". And this was in England or in rest camps far away from the Germans. In the actual fighting line naturally one could forgive anything.

My last few hours in the war were spent in front of a wood near Cambrai. At least, I think so, but I had jettisoned my map case three days before when the NCO who acted as my bearer and runner had most of his head blown off.

The Germans had massed three or four times our gunpower for their March offensive on a narrow front and we had been shelled continuously for three days and nights, about every third shell containing mustard or phosgene gas. Two of my four guns had been hit and over half of my men were casualties, a lot of them from gas. It is quite impossible to keep a gas mask on continuously for twenty-four hours. Your face swells up inside the mask, your lips develop huge cracks and you can't hold the huge clumsy mouthpiece between your teeth with bleeding, cracked lips. Every one of us survivors could feel the burns of mustard gas and we were pretty well out on our feet. So I concentrated our survivors on two guns which fortunately were only twenty yards apart.

During the night our infantry, which was in two or three waves, a thousand or so yards in front of us, came back through our position. An officer in the first wave spoke to me. I thought he said they were merely being relieved by other troops who should have passed me by now going the other way. I must have completely misunderstood him, or he didn't know what was happening himself. Some phosgene gas shells were coming over so we both had on our gas masks. Besides, the infantry always ran for a couple of hundred yards when passing guns that were being shelled and answering back. Quite right too. If it was a limited retreat or a straightening of the line, I should have received orders by runner to try to move my surviving guns back, together with the F.W.D. lorries and tractors to pull them. The tractors were always kept two or three miles in the rear, out of range of the enemy gunfire.

Eventually the last wave of infantry passed us, and then the pickets, who had been keeping up a fast rate of rifle fire to give the Germans the impression that the line was fully held. That, or earlier, was the moment I and my lads should have gone too.

But by now dawn was breaking and we could see to our left what looked through our field glasses like a long line of lorries, three or four miles away and coming down the road that would bring them to within 200 yards of our position. Here was God's gift of a target, and it would soon be in range. Our twenty-five pounders were in a gully and the enemy could not see us so I decided to let the convoy come much nearer and knock out as many lorries as we could before we ran back to the wood where I hoped our infantry was.

I guessed that these road vehicles intended to stop level with our gully and decant their soldiery quickly into it. Officers on both sides were provided with large scale outline duplicated maps probably covering only a few square miles and our gully had been prominently marked upon mine.

What I did not know then was that the Germans were also advancing along our gully on foot to the right of us. Again it is almost certain that they did not know that we were there. They thought that there were no British in front of the wood and they were obviously coming along the gully which was roughly parallel to the wood to take up their positions facing the wood.

I had posted half a dozen chaps with rifles, all I could spare, to watch our right flank along the gully.

It was obvious that we had not been spotted from the air and when the first lorry was only about 600 yards off we opened fire like blazes. The first couple of shells gave us the range and then it was almost impossible to miss. The third lorry must have contained explosives because it blew up and effectively blocked the road for those behind it. And those behind it could not turn around in the narrow road – so for what seemed like hours all hell was let loose. But it was probably more like twenty or twenty-five minutes. The German infantry were well trained. The chaps from the unhit lorries jumped down, spread out, crouched down and came towards us.

We had not been shelled for some hours and I now realized that the enemy would be moving his gun positions forward, probably to our gully, but pointing the other way of course! As soon as we opened fire we were spotted by the Germans advancing along the gully towards our right, and these chaps on our right were much nearer and doubtless much more numerous than those in front. As they were coming along the bottom of the gully they were largely in single file so my few chaps could delay them but not halt them. And now they were leaving the gully and advancing in open order. I had made up my mind what to do – namely to keep on firing until we were on the point of being overwhelmed either from in front or behind, or both, and then give each man the chance of either surrender or make a run for it. The moment duly arrived, and I did just that. I had already warned the surviving NCOs what I was going to do; I was going to run.

179

The Germans knew of course that we should have to surrender or run within a matter of minutes and I think a fairly senior officer, a captain or major, must have gone right to the front of his men to take charge. Because then happened a fine example of the chivalry of war.

Directly we started to run and came out from the gully into the open a German officer, 100 yards or so away, jumped up, turned round to face his men, waved his arms and shouted an order. I glimpsed this as I ran 150 yards from him. He was obviously ordering his men to cease fire and let us get away. The firing almost ceased, and he was waving us on. He was deliberately risking his life. At that moment of stress and fear one of our chaps could easily have shot him almost at point blank range. He turned to his own men and stopped the firing, an heroic gesture for which he was probably afterwards courtmartialled. I was running hard, soaking with sweat I remember, when something hit me in the back, not very hard and fortunately striking my Sam Browne. It was probably a ricochet or even a small piece of rock splintered by a bullet. Or so the doctors thought afterwards. At any rate the jagged holes in my Sam Browne corresponded with the marks which are still on my back.

It may not have been much, but it was enough to knock me out. I was already all in. And the really unfortunate part was that I collapsed into a mustard gas shellhole. I was certainly there for the next twenty-four hours while the battle raged around me, probably much longer, I don't know. The first thing I remember, as I began my story by saying, is being on a dead-waggon. I came to again as I was being examined by a doctor, almost certainly at the Casualty Clearing Station.

Afterwards I have hazy recollections of being fed through a tube, because my lips were split wide open in deep gashes and even to have the tube inserted between them was painful enough to bring me partly back to consciousness. And from time to time I seemed to know I was in a train, doubtless heading for a French port for transport to England.

The first time I really came to was when I was back in England with a burning sensation in my mouth and throat. I learned that I was in a hospital train. Hospital trains used to travel very slowly and would always be stopping at stations where the VAD girls would climb in and distribute tea, coffee, cigarettes, buns, and so on to the wounded soldiery. They were not, however, allowed to enter the compartments marked "Dangerously Wounded". I was in one of these, but a VAD girl did come in, presumably not seeing the notice. I doubt if she had ever seen before an unconscious man with his face puffed up to about twice its normal size and with grease all over his lips, which were cracked about a quarter of an inch wide. She tried to push some hot tea through. She scalded me, of course, and I came round. She was hastily removed, but I had come to for good, and from this point on began to take interest in my life again.

About eighteen months later my immediate superior, Major (acting Colonel) Longden came to see me in hospital. I had not seen him for three days prior to the incident I have just described probably owing to the heavy barrage which preceded the German attack. He told me that he had sent me orders to withdraw with or without the serviceable guns but obviously the runner became a casualty on the way.

EPILOGUE

LIKE Don Quixote, I have tilted my lance at many windmills, with failure and success about equally mixed. I have not stopped nor intend to let my brain atrophy.

This is the joy of being alive and disciplining oneself to use one's capabilities and energies. That is why I put the fable of Hercules at the beginning of this book.

I am sad for those who do not steel themselves to "have a go". They miss so much and the field is so wide and open today. It is always better to have tried and lost than never to have tried at all, and looking forward not backward keeps the mind and body young and fresh.

Today I know of no better words for myself than Edna St. Vincent Millay's poem:

> *I burn my candle at both ends;*
> *It will not last the night;*
> *But ah! my foes and oh! my friends —*
> *It gives a lovely light.*